THE POWER OF
FAITH

How the Love of God Found Me

Frank D. Tigue

ISBN 978-1-961227-54-5 (paperback)
ISBN 978-1-961227-55-2 (digital)

FDT POWER OF FAITH PRESS
fdtlaw@ymail.com
(501) 463-1283

Printed in the United States of America

To Angel Elizabeth Howell---truly an
angel in every sense of the word.

CONTENTS

ACKNOWLEDGEMENT

Jordan Branch, Ella Sanchez, Beth Oliver, and the friendly professional staff at Clever Page Media Literary Agency. By divine intervention, these individuals took me under their wing to assist me in the re-publication of this manuscript as well as the publication of my second book, *The Search for Miri: A Profound Adventure of Faith*. I am truly indebted to their time and expertise.

PROLOGUE

In my life, I have always been a humble man of modest means. I found challenges, struggled, but somehow endured. I always thought my future would be practicing law or delving into politics. However, when God appears to talk to you, you give Him your undivided attention to discern what is being said.

Hence, I need to define *why* I am writing a book about subjects as intense as God and faith. I have no background in faith, nor do I attend church on a regular basis. However, the world in which we live has become hateful and polarized. Our country itself has become a bastion of selfishness, ego, materialism, and bitterness. Likewise, it is sowing seeds that can result in even more polarization and violence than has ever existed in history. People have trouble getting along and finding any solution to seemingly simple problems. The very survival of our society is at stake. Someone needs to provide a voice to change society's direction.

The circular course my life has taken can only be explained in one way. God has been the one who has been leading me. God is taking me down the path He feels I need to go. Due to fortuitous events, fate has interrupted plans of practicing law. My life has taken alternative routes that led me to one conclusion: I love God with all my heart, and I know He loves me. God needed me to be a voice for Him with law just being a secondary afterthought. The love of God has truly found me.

I want this book to make readers aware that I, as one person, cannot solve or have the answers to every problem on my own. It is up to readers to convey to others that faith and compromise will deliver society out of the jaws of self-interest and despair. What one person cannot accomplish, the multitude working together can cast a blanket over, even in the darkest conditions.

There needs to be a voice to lift ordinary people above this despondency. There needs to be a voice to show that, as President Franklin Roosevelt stated, all anyone must fear is fear itself. With God, all things are possible. Without Him, all things can be hopelessly lost, even the human psyche and spirit.

Even if there is one person touched by this literary work, then I have fulfilled God's purpose. Sometimes it feels as though I am not communicating at all. The words ushering from my lips are clearly my own. However, they emanate from another source: one clearly not mine. It is my destiny to try to instill this feeling on all those receptive and who will listen.

It is easy to be afraid when this spirit takes control. One is generally apprehensive at things one does not quite understand. I used to be that way when I first felt surrendering control. Now I welcome this feeling because I know that God's spirit is the one moving me. This means that wherever I go and whatever I do, God is surrounding and protecting me. It is my sincere hope that others can begin to feel the same way and to understand God's awesome power.

The subject matter in this book is broken down succinctly for the benefit and understanding of the readers. I begin chronologically with my birth and boyhood years. I follow that with my education. I then discuss personal tragedies- the death of my father (my hero), two failed marriages, closing down, the attempts to start my law practice again, and finally how God intervened every step of the way. Primarily, God wanted me to not just be aware He existed through these tumultuous times, but He also loved me like no one in this world could love another. He wanted me to know that if I loved Him in return, many blessings would come my way. Surprisingly, these blessings did not result in returning to practice law but supported my livelihood and very survival.

For those readers who are not sure about their faith or feel they have lost their way, I welcome and even encourage them to read this book. Even if the reader strongly believes, this book will reaffirm what I have discovered: God will always provide you what you need, not necessarily what you want. Knowing that God's mighty spirit is near you is an awe-inspiring feeling to have. My life is forever changed by this feeling. People can see it vividly in the way I talk and carry myself. Finally, do not be afraid: this book and God's spirit may just change your life forever.

CHAPTER 1

MY BIRTH:
UNDERSTANDING MY ROOTS

The first blessing ever bestowed on me occurred on October 26, 1961, a time when there was very much a sense of direction and optimism. John F. Kennedy, who was the president at the time, had assumed the reins of government. He had announced policies, like space exploration, that were taking the country through uncharted waters. There was a sense of excitement as to what could be accomplished. President Kennedy remarked that such a direction should be undertaken not because the policies were easy but because they were hard. The sky would be the limit as to what man could achieve if he just set his mind to it and made the commitment.

It was on October 26 that I breathed my first breath of life; I was born at Ball Memorial Hospital in Muncie, Indiana--the youngest son of two children. I have an older brother named John. He was born on March 2, 1960. Notably though, we were the offspring of very ordinary yet caring, principled, and hardworking parents. It truly saddens me that many children today do not receive the kind of nurturing, structure, and discipline I received during my youth.

Baby Photo

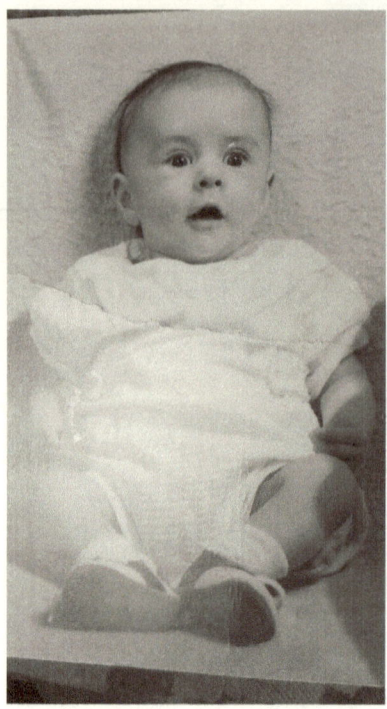

This photo was taken shortly after my birth circa late 1961-early 1962.

My parents have always been and continued to be the driving force in what I have accomplished and what direction my life has taken. Though they did not attend church regularly, their mannerisms conveyed they had a very strong faith and belief in God. Not only was their faith strong, but their devotion to their roles (providing for themselves and their family) was also a paramount aspect in their lives.

By way of background, my father's name was Floyd William Tigue. He was born and raised in Southwest Arkansas (Glenwood/ Amity) on August 18, 1938. He came from a big family---having four brothers and three sisters. As he was growing up, my father's family lived in a difficult time. Arkansas was an impoverished state. There were limited opportunities for anyone living at that time in that locale. Nevertheless, my father was determined to succeed. As he got older, he felt that with limited opportunities, he had to migrate elsewhere to explore a better economic climate and obtain a better paying job. In his late teens, he felt the most prudent decision was to venture north. With just the clothes on his back and some spare change for a sandwich and something to drink, he hitchhiked to East Central Indiana. His eventual destination was Muncie, Indiana. He stayed with a family friend (an older woman referred to as Grandma Barlow) where he began looking for employment. My father was the type that would take any job offered. While he did not finish school, my father had an aptitude that included fixing things, such as vehicles and appliances, and resolving electrical problems. Most importantly, my father had an exemplary work ethic.

My father

This photo of my father, Floyd William Tigue, holding my
National Honor Society plaque was taken circa 1978.

In his quest to find gainful employment, he traveled to Yorktown, Indiana, to try to get work at the Marsh Supermarkets warehouse. Specifically, he hitchhiked (he still had no vehicle at the time) and did this continually. However, when he was told there was no employment, he did not give up. He journeyed out there a few times. This persistence paid off because he eventually received employment as a forklift driver. He held this position for thirty-four years until his death in 1990.

Along with his work ethic, my father was a dedicated and loving family man. He loved his wife but was committed to the best possible rearing of his children. This education did not just begin and end with discipline. My father took an active role in the lives of his boys.

My father frequently ventured outside into the side yard to be with John and me. He would take a baseball bat and "hit flies" to us. He would also take us fishing when he was able. Additionally, there were trips to the Delaware County Fair and the amusement park, Kings Island, in Ohio. For vacations, my father would drive the family to Arkansas to visit his mother and family. Moreover, we would journey to Kentucky to visit my mother's family. All these activities were sandwiched between his responsibilities of work and a hobby (others may call it a necessity to furnish more food for the family) he enjoyed to no end: gardening.

However, my father also possessed a deeply spiritual side. When I was in my elementary school years, I remember my father reading the Bible to my brother. These readings did not occur frequently with me. I suppose it was because my brother was older, so he was first in line for this indoctrination. Moreover, I observed my father manifest this spirituality in common, everyday recreational activities. He had a love for the early sound of country music. He would play albums on an old record player. One of his favorite artists was Johnny Cash, but he had a love for Hank Williams, Sr. as well.

My father also had two guitars, an acoustic and an electric. When he would play a certain album, he would strum one of the guitars and try to sing with the song on the record. While the notes were often off-key and the singing almost monotonous, I know for certain my father derived a high degree of enjoyment and pleasure from this activity. Finally, the Gospel songs of Hank Williams (like "I Saw the Light") were the ones that sounded clearer and more refreshing.

My mother stood in contrast to my father. She was born and raised in South Central Kentucky, near Stearns. Her birthday was May 2, 1940. She had two sisters. She eventually met and married my father and also relocated to East Central Indiana. After marriage, my parents purchased a house and a couple of lots six miles east of Muncie, Indiana, near Selma. This property was in a very quiet and rural area. The area was very conducive to raising a family with minimal disruptions or adverse influences.

Beulah May Tigue née Crabtree was a very quiet woman. Furthermore, she did not work as it was of more pertinent value to my parents that she stayed at home to look after my brother and me. I also feel as if that role at that time was one that was Christian and society-approved and mandated--- the father worked while the mother stayed home with the kids. While she was quiet, she was a loving mother and sensed what she needed to say and do to raise us on the right path.

My mother

This photo of my mother, Beulah May Tigue, standing in our backyard
was taken early 70s. To the left is the back porch where we had our
New Zealand White rabbits. Over her left shoulder is an additional
room that my father built onto the house in the late 60s or early 70s.

Even though she never worked outside the home, her days were
filled with many responsibilities. She always made sure John and I
got ready for school and did not miss the bus. She provided snacks
when we returned home. Not to mention she made little dinners later
in the evenings so we did not go hungry.

During the day, we had a variety of animals she would feed.
At any one time, we would always have at least one dog fenced in
outside. We did not have a farm, but we did have the space to raise a
few chickens and ducks. While many of these animals were outside,
we had a few rabbits on the back porch in cages. She loved to take the
time to make sure the needs of these animals were met.

Despite my mother being busy with her responsibilities, she was
able to spend quality time with me. These memories I cherish and

will always remember. Sometimes, when I reflect on my life, these memories appear surreal. God was beginning to bless me in simple ways during those years. I did not really realize these were blessings at the time.

My mother took the time to play in the yard with me. Whether it was playing catch with a baseball or softball or playing croquet, I knew she loved me and wanted to share her time with me. However, it did not stop there. We had two big walnut trees in the side yard by our driveway. During the autumn months, these leaves would slowly change. Not only was it extraordinary for me to see these leaves fall, but my mother and I would also take the time and effort to see how many of these leaves we could catch in our bare hands. While it did not end up being many, it was the thrill and being with my mother that was so extraordinary.

I have one last comment about my father. One day in the kitchen (I had to be no more than seven or eight), he asked me the question all young children typically got asked early in childhood. He asked. "Son, what do you want to be when you grow up?" I told him I wanted to become the president of the United States. Hence, at an early age I had a sense that I wanted to help people. Likewise, being a lawyer was a typical prerequisite for political life. To be president, I would have to become a lawyer. Being from such a humble background, I had no example or role model to direct me on how to get there.

However, God started to bless me at a very early age just by being born. Unfortunately, I did not even see it at the time. It was as if I had blinders over my eyes. As time progressed, God had a plan for me. God wanted me to be in His life. Yet He, like a good parent, wanted me to learn about Him on my own. He provided a path but prodded me to go down it, learning from any diversion. The adventure of my faith and love of God was just beginning.

CHAPTER 2

MY BOYHOOD:
LOVING FAMILY AND FRIENDS

Our Home

I n the regular course of affairs in one's life, it is unusual that one suddenly arrives at an endpoint directly from the beginning. My struggle to find myself, and ultimately my love of God and His love for me, took many different twists and turns during my life. This realization developed as I started to get older and mature. Yet each story has a beginning. It is best for me to start with my boyhood years.

However, a pertinent question asked is how my parents met. The fact that they got together at all was a divine gift in itself. The very answer supplies the emotion one can similarly feel in the most riveting romance novel. I already mentioned my father staying with Grandma Barlow in Muncie. While I did not know or remember this woman, she played an integral role in bringing my parents together.

Grandma Barlow was, in fact, connected to my mother's side of the family. She was my maternal grandmother's stepmother. My maternal grandmother's name was Esta Crabtree whom I will refer to as Granny. Grandma Barlow was married to Granny's father.

During the time my father resided with Grandma Barlow, he started corresponding with my mother. My mother lived near the coal-mining town of Stearns, Kentucky. It was a tourist area but, like Arkansas, it was a very economically destitute locale. Eventually, after a few letters, my mother journeyed to Indiana to visit my father. Obviously, their relationship clicked. After the third visit, my parents decided to get married. They married on June 2, 1959.

After the births of my brother and me, my family was far from being wealthy and without needs. We had consistent struggles throughout our lives. Like many people in today's society, we endured from paycheck to paycheck. Since my father was the only breadwinner, that fact amplified our struggles. My father's employment at the Marsh Supermarkets warehouse was a tremendous blessing. With the wage and the benefits, the job allowed our family to obtain our necessities. Those necessities included typical expenses, such as electricity and groceries. Sometimes, we had a little extra for vacations and other activities outside of the home. I do not remember much about our health care, but I know we were covered.

A great benefit was the fact that we owned our little home. It was very small. As you opened the front door, there was a very small thin carpeted living room. It was simple with little furnishings. There was a couch, two chairs, and a very small black-and-white television. Watching this little black-and-white TV was the main source of indoor recreation as I was growing up.

Straight ahead, there was an open doorway that led to a small kitchen. The kitchen was extremely small with a table and four chairs. It also had a stove, refrigerator, and a kitchen sink. The only bathroom with just a toilet and a bathtub (no shower) was located to the immediate right after entering this room. The kitchen area was where my mother did her cooking. She might not be the best cook in the world to many, but I would give a lot for a homemade meal from her, like her meatloaf or her pinto beans and fried potatoes. Sometimes the simplest things, while not the very best, are so good because of the love that goes into them. My mother and my father had so much love to give us and to all others they knew.

Parallel to the open doorway and straight back, there was the door that led to the back porch. At one time, this area had a few New Zealand White rabbits in cages that my mother loved tending to. Additionally, there was a wild rabbit we found injured that my mother and I tried to nurse back to health. Likewise, there was a guinea fowl that had injured its leg. We kept the wild rabbit and the guinea on the porch and took care of both of them. Our whole family had a genuine love and fondness for any kind of animal.

Adjacent to the living room and off to the left in the corner was a very short hallway. The first door on the left was the bedroom of my brother and me. At the end of this open hallway was the bedroom of my parents. Looking back, this area was so incredibly small, I wonder now how it was able to accommodate a family of four like ours.

With life and technology much simpler at the time, we had many more limitations on the choices of what we could do. I have already mentioned the black-and-white television in our living room. When we were not watching it or listening to a radio or records on a record player---which was popular at that time---we were outside engaging in some kind of outdoor activity.

Outside, my brother and I had a broad array of activities to choose from. Attached to our homemade garage my father constructed was a basketball goal. Even on rainy days, going out and shooting free throws in the muddy gravel was an eventful part of our lives. Being in Indiana, and the home of Hoosier Hysteria, this activity had to be our first source of recreation. However, there were other activities that were options for us. With the large area on the side of the house, we would toss a football or even play football games. I even broke my collarbone as a teenager during one of our impromptu games. Along with my father hitting a baseball to us, we also played baseball games. Unfortunately, as we grew and our hitting power increased, it became imprudent to continue since we either hit our house with the baseball or managed to lose the baseball in the weeds in the neighboring fields.

There were other outside activities we could select. We could set up the course for games of croquet. At times we had a net where we could play either badminton or volleyball. However, these activities always carried added significance when our parents took some time away from their busy routine to spend with us.

Frank and Brother (1968)

This photo of my brother John and me was taken circa 1968. We are on a swing set by the two walnut trees beside the short driveway. In the extreme lower right of the photo is our lane which was just gravel at that time. There is a grass growing in the middle of this lane. Additionally, there was no development across the lane or further down toward the end at that time. There was only Mr. Charles Hunt's house at the end of the lane.

While our house and land around it was so small and simple, God was beginning to provide the blessings to sustain us through the years. My boyhood years had to be the most memorable in my life. But God had not yet revealed His true self to me. The foundation was there, but the knowledge and maturity to understand were not apparent. It started with the place I called home. However, it was the family that I had and the friends who crossed my path that helped mold my mindset for the blessings that were to come.

My Family and Friends

During any person's life, his or her character and temperament are largely molded by the people encountered during the life of this person. Whether family members or friends or even brief acquaintances, these individuals play a significant role in what the person essentially becomes. On top of that aspect is the role that God takes in this whole process. The extent of God's involvement is determinative of how blessed that person will become.

I like to compare this thought to planting and trying to grow something. My faith and spirituality are seeds, the family and friends are the sunlight and moisture conducive for growth, and God is the ultimate fertilizer if allowed to work.

As a kid, I only knew God superficially. I could not say I really knew him. However, God provided me the opportunity to be blessed with visits to caring family along with being surrounded by caring friends and teachers. Through these interactions and my uncomplicated way of life, I was slowly establishing the direction my life was to follow.

Along with my parents, my more distant family played an integral role in my maturation and the journey toward God. Because my father was from Arkansas, I had a huge family there that I could bond with. Additionally, my mother had her family in Kentucky that I similarly could learn from and mature.

Almost every summer, my father would take at least a week off work. During this time, our family would travel to Kentucky, then to Arkansas. We would generally stop in Kentucky first to visit my mother's family. Afterward, we continued the rest of the way to Arkansas. Our first stop was Stearns, Kentucky. We visited my grandmother, Esta Crabtree, first. My grandfather, Charles Crabtree, died when I was very young, so I do not remember him well. Granny would always supply us with a bed to sleep in along with enough country-cooked food to feed us many times over. She would cook big breakfasts with homemade biscuits and gravy, bacon and eggs, toast, coffee, milk, and orange juice. For lunch, she would make hamburgers or simple bologna sandwiches (sometimes, double-deckers) fit for royalty.

Granny Crabtree and Grandpa

My Granny Crabtree and Grandpa (Charles Crabtree)
was taken sometime in the mid to late 60s.

My mother had two sisters (Thelma and Brenda). Each of my aunts would likewise make simple homemade meals for us. Each of her sisters had daughters. Thelma had three daughters, and Brenda had two. Thelma lived near Stearns, but Brenda was farther away, on her farm near Pine Knot. (Brenda lived in Springdale, near Cincinnati, before moving to Pine Knot. Our family visited her family there once in the early 1970's before she moved.) We would visit each aunt and spend a lot of time playing with our cousins.

Our visits were memorable in a straightforward way. Other than visiting and talking, we journeyed to such locales like Tombstone Junction (a Western-style amusement park with a train featuring big name country music entertainers) or Cumberland Falls or even went fishing when we could. In my heart, I always yearned for those trips. While we did watch a little on televisions Grandma Crabtree and Aunt Thelma had, most of the time was spent talking to each other and playing when we were not eating. We did not do much, but we understood the importance of family and the need for family interaction and caring.

Our final stop was Amity, Arkansas. The main gathering place was at my grandmother's house (Grandma Barbara Tigue). It was there where all members of the family would congregate. Whether it was a visit by one of my father's siblings or even more distant relatives, each family member (and family friend) would frequently visit our family matriarch; at the same time, all of us would be able to see how everyone else was doing.

Our visits to Arkansas, like Kentucky, were very simple. Most of the time was spent talking and visiting. However, on the Fourth of July, we would ignite a few fireworks. At times, we even had an opportunity to find a creek and go swimming, go "tubing"-floating down the river in an inflated innertube- or go fishing. On a few rare occasions, we even had the opportunity to go horseback riding.

Grandma Tigue lived on a farm of sorts. She had cows to milk and eggs to gather from the chickens she had. From year to year, she also raised a garden with a variety of items she planted.

Additionally, she had a horse and a few ponies. I see where my father established his work ethic. Grandma Tigue was always spending time working around her home. I guess it was a necessity because of the impoverished setting she lived in. I also think it was because raising so many children could be costly in itself.

As with any family, at times you are too busy surviving to face your spirituality. Nevertheless, God clearly wanted me to establish an essential link with my family. He wanted me to see how important it was to have a bond with my family that nurtured my spirituality. It would be from that interaction that God's love and guidance would begin to affect every aspect of my life. God had only begun to plant the seeds of His love. I had not yet realized what was happening. My friends and schoolteachers, likewise, slowly nurtured God's very slow emergence into my life.

Each day, every living person crosses paths with others albeit it can be on a fleeting basis. It is impossible for me to name everyone who interacted with me since boyhood who had some effect on what I have become. Fortunately, there are those individuals whose impact left an indelible mark, especially on how God's love found me. It is those individuals I will mention briefly.

My very first best friends were two brothers and their mother and father who lived a few houses from where I lived. The father was a pastor (Russell), the mother a housewife (Rose). They had two sons, Jim and Tom Hanson. Jim and Tom were around the same age as my brother and me. We only lived close for a brief time. The fact that their father was a pastor and that they were regular churchgoers stands out in my memory. Sometimes, I wonder what role God would have had at an earlier time if we would have been neighbors longer. God has significant reasons why things happen the way they do. This family ultimately moved to Wisconsin.

As a boy growing up, the rural locale of our home sometimes made it very difficult to meet good friends. One of the first I remember was a friend who lived up the tiny lane from me. His name is Keith Davis. We often got together to play basketball on the simple garage hoop I mentioned earlier, and we played peewee ball in his yard. It would turn out that Keith would become a star player on the high school basketball team.

Keith and I shared a love for all sports, but his main love was basketball. We were both extremely competitive as well. While I believe I was not as talented as a basketball player as he was, I wanted to funnel my energies and competitive zeal into an area I could excel and accomplish in: academics. I thought in my mind I could never have the innate sports talent he possessed. However, I did believe I had a very warm source of intelligence that, if nurtured, I could become anything I wanted to be, even an attorney.

I was very timid when I was a boy. I rarely said anything unless I was spoken to. This characteristic made it difficult for me to interact with people. However, my love of learning helped circumvent this trait. I studied, received good grades, and began to establish myself academically.

My schoolteachers generally reflected that they saw a lot of potential in me. They made attempts to nurture my intelligence. Realizing this potential, they dedicated themselves to focusing on teaching me individually. With this focus, the result was clear: I was always on the honor roll and my primary goal was to become the high school valedictorian.

I had one particular teacher who stood out significantly: Mrs. Betty McCafferty. She was as kind-hearted a woman to anyone who had ever met her. She taught me classes in general business, accounting, and typing. While seemingly a gruff woman, she had a sensitivity and a heart of gold.

For a National Honor Society banquet, I informed her (as the teacher sponsor) I had nothing formal to wear. When I said that I lacked the attire, she arranged to take me out to the Muncie Mall. It was there where she purchased a new suit for me. While I might not have realized it as a blessing then, through the years I began to realize how important a blessed gesture that was to me. God was slowly knocking at my door to gain entry into my life and heart. I had not really begun to say prayers at this point.

It did not end there, though. When it became closer to the time for me to graduate, Mrs. McCafferty furnished me with a card. It was simplistic in tone, but far overreaching in thought. The card was of a young man wearing a dress shirt with his right leg elevated on a boulder. The young man was looking across a body of water. The card had the saying, "There is nothing beyond the reach of determination." It was that simple act of kindness and the contents of that particular card that left a lasting impression on my heart to this date. Through it all, even though I did not see the actual strength at the time (but I knew He was there), God was creating his fertilizing mark on my spiritual maturation. Through God, all things are possible, including becoming a lawyer.

Finally, I have one more friend to mention whose friendship started when I was a boy. It endured through the years. Even to this date, we continue to have close contact and a connection that is exemplary. I am convinced God has made this friendship durable through the years because of the subtle messages I receive from him through time. It was when I was with him and his mother a few years ago that I saw how much God really loved me and always has. His name is Darrell King. Whereas Keith Davis lived midway down our lane, Darrell lived closer to the highway at the start of our lane. He and his family welcomed me into their lives and home at a young age. Many days we would play games together, whether badminton or croquet outside or a tabletop basketball game I purchased many years ago inside. If there were one family that I am convinced had God's glory, it would be his family.

I have learned many lessons from him over the years. These lessons entail how to live, love, and interact with others. The most important lesson he taught was when I quit one job because of pressure for performance, he told me to not leave where I was until I knew where I was going. This simply meant never quitting a job unless you had another one already in place.

As I reflect, I have begun to realize the point where I started. I lacked any foundation for my love for God other than praying for survival. Survival meant finding employment to put food on my table and a roof over my head. However, with my birth followed by where I was raised, God was gently and gradually fertilizing my heart with His love for me. I never knew it at the time.

God helped furnish the blessings I needed to transition from survival to actual spiritual growth. From my home to my family to my friends, the sunshine had begun to take hold for my spiritual maturation. This maturation and eventual spiritual catharsis further enhanced the growth of God's love for me and my love for Him. Most excitedly, the fertilizing journey into the power of faith had just started and the best was yet to come.

Photos of Lane and House

As a traveler ventures out of Muncie on Highway 32 east, he will bypass the small town of Selma. Continuing on Highway 32, this person would observe a big electrical tower right beside the highway. In front of this tower is the little lane of my youth (Northwood Drive). This first picture is a photo of the street sign along with a visual of the beginning of this lane. The lane is roughly paved and is approximately 1/2-mile long. I am including the current photos of the lane and the house to illustrate my most humble roots.

This is another view of the lane from Highway 32. To the right is the large electrical tower. In my early academic years, all the children down the lane would need to catch the bus in this locale. It is important to indicate that the first driveway is the driveway in front of the house where Darrell King and family lived. We spent many moments out in the yard playing badminton or tag. Don and Mary King (Darrell's parents) always welcomed me into their home and made me feel a part of their family. Mary King still lives there.

After reaching the first little curve, you will pass approximately five to seven house on the right. At that point, you reach a slightly elevated point that we would call "the hill". You will then see what is depicted in this photo. You cannot see it in this photo, but the house to the immediate right was where Jim and Tom Hanson lived. Further, about three houses back was where Keith Davis lived. Not really in view yet, the third house on the right is the home where I was raised as a boy. As an incidental note, during most of my youth, none of the houses to the left existed. The serious development only started in the late 70s to early 80s when I was away at school.

In this photo, the house comes clearer into view. The white fence is new since our house was surrounded by a wire fence that my father constructed when I was young.

This photo is even closer to the house. It has been years since anyone in my family lived there. When I was young, the house was white. There was a wire fence all around the house and yard, unlike in this photo. The buildings in the back as well as trees and other clutter also did not exist when I was a boy. Also, there were a few thin evergreens that my father had planted in front of the house next to the fence by the road.

This is a current view of what used to be my old home. When I was a child, this house was painted white. As you walk in the front door was the living room. The second window is where my brother and I had our bedroom. As we got older, we had bunk beds with my bed on top. Finally, the first window closer to the camera is where my parents had their bedroom. There were no trees in the back of the house as shown in this image. Finally, there was a wire fence surrounding the house with a front gate.

This photo is another view of the house. While there was another room added behind my parents' bedroom with a door to enter from and to exit to the garage with access to the kitchen, the window seen at this end is new. Moreover, you can see the driveway. When I was young, Dad had built a garage next to the house. The entire house was painted white too. My father constructed a basketball goal at the front of this garage. My brother and I would spend many moments shooting hoops on this goal. Through time and wear, this garage looks like it has been demolished by the new owners.

This is a current photo of the driveway. During my youth, there was a garage that my father constructed where those cars currently are. There was a basketball goal affixed in front so my brother, my friends, and I could play. The two walnut trees grew to the immediate left from this photo. Almost straight back and a little to the left was a pen that my mother would have chickens, ducks, and rabbits. We also had a fenced in area where we had three dogs: Rover, Friskie, and Tenderfoot. At one time, straight ahead we also had a dog house with a little dog we kept tied up named Caesar.

This photo is a view further down from the house. I believe off center and to the right is one of the walnut trees I refer to in Chapter One. Again, there was a wire fence my father constructed around our house and the accompanying lots. The white fence shown replaces this wire fence. It was this side area that my brother and I would play baseball or football with our friends. It was clear of clutter and mowed.

This photo is a view even further down from the house. My father owned the house and first lot soon after being married. A short time later, he purchased a second lot further down from the house. It is this area of the side yard that was mowed, cleared, and we played baseball and football. There were not many trees or clutter then as you can see in these current photos.

Another view looking down toward our house. It is obvious many more trees have been planted in this area. When I was a boy, this area was clear enabling my brother and I to play an array of sports. To reiterate, when I was a boy, there was no development of the lots to the right. This area was mainly undeveloped and weeds. Only after I went away to college and law school did the development become more pronounced to what it has become today. My father grew his small garden toward the back of this property.

Another view facing the highway almost at the end of the lane.

The final view facing the highway from the end of the lane. The first development in this lane occurred on the left side next to our house. The development started with a few duplexes. I am glad my father had the two lots because that would inhibit any development where I could run free and play.

This image is a photo of the very end of our lane. The house pictured used to be the house of Mr. and Mrs. Charles Hunt. They also had a fence around this property. This fence has been removed through the years. Likewise, the driveway has faded presumably because of non-use. When I was a teenager, I had a mini bike that I would ride up and down the lane as well as around this fenced property.

CHAPTER 3

My Educational Years: How I Sensed God Was Near

My boyhood years developed into a consistent struggle. Mainly, this struggle was economic--my parents having the resources to keep food on the table and bills paid. It is a disconcerting feeling to continually be subjected to that type of stress. Through my childhood and in observation, I was determined to break out of that cycle.

My father realized the importance of getting dressed and heading to work daily. For most of his career with Marsh Supermarkets, he worked second shift. After getting up early in the morning to work in the garden or do other chores (like mowing the grass), he would rest a little then get ready to go to work. After grabbing his brown bag lunch that my mother would prepare, he would say his goodbyes. I would kiss him on the cheek, and he would be out the door.

Using him as a role model, I had to remove myself from this cycle. I did not want to struggle as much in my future. In the back of my mind, I wanted to be president one day. I needed to excel academically to have a chance at that goal. My first goal was to graduate from high school.

I attended a little public school system near Selma, Indiana. The name of that system is the Liberty-Perry School Corporation located in Delaware County. That system included the following schools I attended: Selma Elementary School, Selma Middle School, and Wapahani High School. I never seemed to have a problem academically or with my homework. That aspect was the result of the personal attention and commitment the teachers in that system provided. It was also the result of the constant love and encouragement of my parents and other family members and friends.

On the other hand, I was able to have simple interests outside of school to occupy my time and heart. I watched programs on our black and white television, like *Gilligan's Island* or *Star Trek*. I listened to music either on the radio or record player. However, when cassettes and tape recorders were developed, these advances would replace record players and even 8-track tapes. Finally, most of my time was spent outside. I loved all sports, so I loved shooting the basketball. When my brother and I could, we would arrange either basketball, baseball, or even football games. As a kid, having fun was paramount; unfortunately, God was not visible in my life's picture. My ultimate issue was survival. Recreation supplied an essential outlet from everyday stress and reality. I still felt as if an unseen force was dictating my accomplishments and the course my life was taking.

A highlight of my life was when I received my grades. I was consistently on the all-A honor roll. It was something special to get on the honor roll and get your name in the newspaper. Likewise, this achievement had its rewards. Sometimes, we received ice cream or soda pop, or other treats for that accomplishment.

The greatest blessing in my life to date was yet to come.

As the years progressed, I managed to pass the grades in Selma Elementary and Selma Middle School. I entered Wapahani High School as the last object in my early academic education. Unfortunately, I had no role model to observe. My father dropped out of school in the eighth grade, my mother returned to get a correspondence GED, and my brother dropped out of Wapahani at the beginning of his junior year. Yet there existed something in the back of my mind, prodding me and telling me in subtle ways that I could do this. A voice echoed, "There is nothing beyond the reach of determination." I knew I was in the top few students in my class- the Wapahani Class of 1980.

Although my goal was to become the class valedictorian, I had an obstacle standing in my way. Her name was Nannette Humbert. I knew I was very intelligent and strong academically. However, I did not know if I was the smartest one in my class. The answer was provided in a physics class. I managed to get a better grade than Nannette. With the competitive zeal I learned a while back with my friendship with Keith Davis, I managed to reach my goal of becoming the class valedictorian.

High School Graduation

This photo of me receiving my high school diploma was taken in May 1980. In the photo, Superintendent Melvin Richman is handing me my diploma. Looking on is the high school principal, Tom Childs. At the podium is Wapahani teacher, Julie Ferraro.

My determination resulted in me graduating at the top of my high school class. Naturally, there are perks associated with this accomplishment. I would have to give a valedictory address on graduation day. This achievement was such an overwhelming honor for me.

As a subject of this speech, I mentioned how an invisible force had been guiding our class to this point. We had been moved by some invincible and motivational force that was spurring our accomplishments. Hence, there is little question God was affecting me at a distance, even at that time. While my heart and faith had grown in small increments to get to that point, I had an extensive distance to travel to really comprehend how God was guiding me and nurturing my love for Him.

Finally, what happened after my speech is enlightening in a very obscure but revealing and memorable way. As my family was exiting the high school, a full moon appeared right above the roof of the school. It was as if someone was watching me. God wanted to give me a sign that He was there once I was able to comprehend the significance of this occurrence.

While this graduation was a prize in itself, becoming the class valedictorian led to an even greater prize. This prize was so astronomical; I continue to feel the repercussions today. A wealthy banker in Muncie died, leaving a trust fund. Muncie was the county seat for Delaware County. With this trust fund, he would designate at least one student from each of the Delaware County high schools to receive a full tuition scholarship with a stipend for room and board and books. The name of this prominent banker was Oliver W. Storer. In 1980, each school in our county (approximately nine) had at least one recipient of his valued scholarships. Wapahani High School had two. While Nannette received one from our school, I was very blessed to receive the other. Had I not received this award, I would really question if I would even be able to go to college.

As a result of this blessing, I was given a choice of where to attend college. Ball State University was a common choice for students in our area. However, while I wanted to be close to home, I wanted to be different. After a brief review, I only applied to DePauw University in Greencastle, Indiana.

DePauw University is located on the other side of Indianapolis in West Central Indiana. The small school had established a very strong academic reputation. This reputation was bolstered by the names of prominent people attending this institution. This non-exhaustive list included such persons as former Vice President Dan Quayle, civil rights activist Vernon Jordan, author John Jakes, and cultural anthropologist Margaret Mead. (Most recently, Brad Stevens joined that list. He is currently the head coach of the NBA's Boston Celtics.) Additionally, DePauw was known for its excellent pre-law/political science department.

In the recesses of my mind, I realized this had to be the school to assist my efforts in becoming a lawyer. I needed to receive the necessary training and skills to be accepted into a reputable law school. DePauw University was in a unique position to provide this training for me.

When scholarships like this are given, they are newsworthy. The recipients' names and photos are published in the local newspaper. That was what transpired after my selection. The article ran in both *The Muncie Evening Press* and *The Muncie Star* newspapers.

When I reflect on my past, subtle events have happened that led me to never doubt that God was near me. My mother and I went to the local Selma grocery store after I was chosen. While my mother was inside, I was surprised when a little girl (no more than nine or ten, I guess) came by the car where I was sitting. She had a question to ask me. After we made eye contact, she asked if I was the guy whose name and picture appeared in the newspaper. I answered her affirmatively with a smile. It was then that she asked if she could have my autograph. It was one of the most heartwarming encounters I had experienced in my whole life.

While my goals were slowly coming to fruition, I was on my way to an adventure to attend college. In a very esoteric manner,

God had directed me to the path my life would begin to realize. He wanted me to go to school and mature. He wanted me to learn not just about Him but about life. My goal was to become an attorney. However, God would reveal other plans and goals for me.

CHAPTER 4

COLLEGE AND LAW SCHOOL: A TIME TO QUESTION AND DOUBT BUT ACCOMPLISH GOALS

Throughout my youth, God was slowly fertilizing my seed of faith. He wanted me to be aware He was around if I ever needed Him. It was during my college and law school years that I believe He tempered the sprinkle of His fertilizing hand. Like a good parent, He wanted time and maturity to create in my mind and heart a little doubt of His love and existence. The best way to establish this sentiment was through the nurturing of a proper education. This education included the people I came in contact with and my interaction with them.

I began my trek to DePauw University with the excitement of a newly discovered independence. With my eagerness for knowledge, I was overjoyed at the prospect of learning. I would understand what it was to live on my own. The solitude away from my parents would enable me to study and have necessary experiences resulting from being on my own. I pursued my dream of becoming an attorney, yet I had no role model to look to who had ventured down a similar road before me.

I first drove to DePauw in a 1975 Ford Mustang. It had a worn-out body but was a terrific car. For the first part of my advanced educational journey, it withstood the test of time. Most importantly, this vehicle was a bargain. When my father and I went to a Muncie used car lot during the summer of 1980 to look at vehicles, we discovered this Mustang. I still cannot believe the purchase price- $350.

Upon arrival at school, I relished my first attempt at self-reliance. I was away from home for the first time. I had the ability to find new friends. I began to understand what it took to interact with diverse types of individuals. Even though I had no role model to look to, what really stood out was the fact that I took this journey alone. I did not yet understand this was a false thought; God was with me in every moment of this journey.

The pursuit of my education seemed to be the easiest part of this trek. However, my studies were not without stress. For me, the thrill of learning was like no other. To digest information I did not know previously was incredible. Moreover, as with almost everything, everyone needs time away from the stresses of academic life. The sheer volume of information in any one course could be overwhelming. Having the time away to relax and unwind was imperative.

My ways to unwind initially took an unhealthy course. Like many other colleges, DePauw had a significant Greek system. Fraternities and sororities abound. A hallmark of beginning college was the participation by the new student during rush week. For me, the ultimate highlight was joining a fraternity. Unfortunately, it did not seem that I could really fit in or be stereotyped for any one of the fraternities. I was not really a jock, nor could I be classed as a geek or nerd. The bottom line was not one fraternity invited me for a return visit. It was heart-wrenching for me at that time in my life to be excluded from that type of social interaction. While I was still timid, I consistently desired new friends with the possibility of romance. With this type of ostracism, I never lost the thirst for social interaction. To quench this thirst, I became familiar with the fraternity parties consistently held on campus. To attend these parties, it was customary to drink alcohol. In those days, parties were not significantly regulated. There was easy access to alcohol.

It was not uncommon for a fraternity to throw a kegger, an open party with kegs of beer. In addition to a significant quantity of alcohol, these parties had music and dancing. More importantly, the parties also had a seemingly endless supply of college girls. Through these parties, it was my hope that I would have the opportunity to find and interact with a compatible coed. I guess I had a longing for love and to be loved.

One flaw of my character I have grappled with all my life is my ability to interact with people, especially the opposite gender. These keggers did not really help. I seemed to have gotten lost in drinking more than socializing. At one particular fraternity, I never seemed to leave without becoming inebriated.

Fortunately, God, even at a distance, opened my eyes. During my youth, my father had a drinking problem I denied having existed for the longest time. I saw my father come home in states no living being should see another, especially someone this person loved as much as I loved my father. When I had occasional phone conversations with him, it was impossible not to detect alcohol in his voice. Maybe that was a significant reason why I desired to leave home so badly.

Because of this revelation, my experiences with the fraternity parties were short-lived. Seeing an alcoholic within my family was distasteful in itself. To drink on my own merely compounded that distaste. I hated the way I felt the following day. As a result, my chief focus returned to my studies. Through my own experiences, God was allowing me to learn for myself and experience life on my own.

I was fighting for my economic survival. With my continued focus on studies, I needed an outlet to alleviate academic stress. While visits to my home to see my parents, brother, and friends were frequent, I also turned to the love I had when I was a kid. That love was my continued love for sports. Whether it was college football, college and pro basketball, or some other popular sport, I was a very avid fan. Furthermore, there were certain teams I followed regularly. For example, I was a Los Angeles Lakers fan of basketball. In baseball, I started out as a Cincinnati Reds fan in the 1970s. My sentiment changed close to 1980 when I began following the Los Angeles Dodgers. Finally, in pro football, the Pittsburgh Steelers were my team.

Why I mention that love is significant for me. My life seemed to be reflective of how these teams were doing. In the mid-1970s, the Big Red Machine was winning championships. Likewise, the Steelers also began their Super Bowl runs in the mid-1970s. Finally, the Lakers began their run of NBA titles beginning in 1980 and continuing throughout that decade. During the 1970s, I made my commitment to graduate and become the class valedictorian. It was also during the 1980s that I graduated from DePauw University and Capital University Law School.

With my inquisitive mind, my eagerness to learn ran rampant during my college years. I also began to question God's very existence. Did God truly exist? If so, why was there so much pain and hardship in the world? Why, with good parents like I had, were people afflicted with seemingly insurmountable obstacles, struggles, and even health issues? I was only in the beginning process of discovering those answers. Only by raising those questions would I truly be able to see the blessings God had provided throughout my life. Even at that point, I felt something spiritual; some unseen force was dictating the direction my life headed. God eventually provided the reasons why events unfolded the way they did.

In what seemed surreal at the time, my focus enabled me to complete my degree at DePauw in 1984. I received a bachelor's degree in political science, with minors in psychology and anthropology. DePauw had done an extraordinary job in preparing me for my future. To complete my academic journey, I needed to take the next step: find, attend, and eventually graduate from law school. How would I do that when I did not know the first thing about attending any post-college graduate school?

God always knows your plans and what you need, even though you may not. My next goal consisted of finding a law school to attend. Since my parents had never made a commitment like that, they had no genuine advice or way that could help. They could only offer me love, support, and encouragement. The rest was left to me.

My initial inquiry would be, because of our socioeconomic situation, whether we even had the finances to undertake the bold endeavor of me attending law school. Such an excursion might even need to be delayed for me to gather the financial support for such a trek. I researched some schools. One, in particular, caught my attention: Capital University Law School in Columbus, Ohio. I reviewed the profile for this school and felt something pull me in that direction. Capital University was an up-and-coming school, establishing notable academic credentials. The school was also located in a big city. I had never lived in such a vicinity before. This school would provide a unique opportunity for me along with many challenges.

Capital University Law School was the only law school I applied to. It was the only law school to accept my credentials. After discussing attending law school with my father, we felt I needed to try to get some form of loan or financial assistance. Furthermore, I also needed to sit out a year before leaving to work and provide help with finances. As my thoughts were focused on my economic survival, I was willing to do whatever it took to get to my last and ultimate objective: becoming an attorney.

I was able to secure student loans. I was able to mentally prepare during the year that I sat out. This mental preparation was essential in helping me establish a focus on this unique journey. Law school was like no other school anyone could attend. I knew I would make it. There was little doubt when I made the leap in summer of 1985. I had gotten so close; I could not afford to turn back now.

Law school used a method of teaching that I had never heard of or had been exposed to: The Socratic method. Despite this method, law school had its simplicity for me. I read court cases and gleaned various information about them. I wrote this information in a case brief. This information included the facts of the case, how the case arrived in court, what the court decided, and the rationale of the case. While some cases were incredibly long and intricate, diligence in my observation helped me to separate, formulate, and articulate the right information in the briefs.

Utilizing the Socratic method was fascinating for me. Basically, this method used the function of asking various questions, funneling to answers, and then devising other questions from prior answers to eventually arrive at the ultimate answer desired. This method was named after the ancient Greek philosopher who employed it to assist his students in reaching important answers to common philosophical issues. It did wonders in helping to develop a rational and analytical thought process.

Gaining familiarity with this method and its functions, I began to use this method in common everyday issues. I sincerely believe I subconsciously began using it in my quest to discern God's love and existence. Only by asking questions can you arrive at essential answers, provoking more needed questions. Woefully, I did not yet appreciate the answers that would be provided in God's time, not my time.

With my diligence, focus, and preparation, I graduated from Capital University Law School in 1988. Along with the law degree, the totality of my education undoubtedly prepared me mentally for my future. While my next goal was to obtain a law license, I could not, in any way, fathom how my college and law school years had opened my mind and heart to God's very existence and love. Realizing this fact, God would begin anew to fertilize my spiritual maturation for the journey that was to come.

Law School Graduation

This photo of my parents, my brother, and me was taken in May 1988. On this date, I received my law school degree from Capital University Law School. The photo was taken in my upstairs apartment on Mohawk Street in Columbus, Ohio.

CHAPTER 5

BECOMING AN ATTORNEY:
THE CAST OF AN
OMINOUS SHADOW

Death of My Hero

God is always around to lend His hand when needed. All one must do is merely turn to Him and ask. Not only should one give praise to Him when times are good, any believer or one who aspires to secure His love should also come to Him when times are bad. While most of my life was a struggle, I had little in unforeseen tragedies up to, and including, my years in law school.

The year 1988 was an incredibly special and memorable year for me. During that year, the Los Angeles Lakers were on their way to repeating as NBA champions in a seven-game showdown with the Detroit Pistons. Moreover, the Los Angeles Dodgers would win their epic World Series battle with the Oakland Athletics later in the year. The first game culminated in one of the most memorable at-bats I had ever seen: Kirk Gibson's walk off home run in the bottom of the ninth that excited the crowd and propelled the Dodgers to the eventual series victory. But 1988 was also the year that I graduated from Capital University Law School.

During my graduation, I received a blessing that was touching and never expected. A group of teachers from Wapahani traveled from Selma to Columbus to see me. They were excited and wanted to share in this accomplishment. No graduate from Wapahani, in my recollection, had gone to law school and graduated, especially someone from my modest means and background.

Mr. Kenneth Brown, my former math teacher at Wapahani, led the group. This group conveyed their congratulations at what I accomplished. Additionally, this visit inspired Mr. Brown to write a moving letter to the editor of a Muncie newspaper reflecting what I had accomplished. I guess God wanted to let that area know what success I had established in my career venture.

Using this inspiration as a stepping stone, I set out to accomplish my last objective before becoming an attorney: passing the Ohio state bar examination. Any state bar exam is unlike any test anyone can take. While each individual state may have variations, generally the exam is a two- or three-day ordeal. Two days are set aside for essay questions dealing with state law; the third day is a multistate version with multiple choice questions dealing with common multistate legal subjects. The Ohio exam was a three-day test.

The bar exam questions and format are not difficult in themselves. What makes it so difficult is, especially for the multiple-choice questions, there may be more than one right answer. It is the responsibility of the exam taker to pick what answer is more correct than the others. This type of exam is the hardest type to pass. You may think you picked the right answer, but noting a certain fact or the wording will eliminate that answer from consideration.

I felt with the proper preparation, there would be little doubt I would pass. To assist in this preparation, I enrolled in a typical bar review course. This course covered all relevant subjects as well as gave tips on how to write essays and pick the right answers for multiple-choice questions. More importantly, I would have the ability to take this course again in the unlikely event I did not pass.

I first sat for the Ohio exam in the summer of 1988. To pass, one needs to accumulate 270 out of 360 points. There is little room for error. Unfortunately, you can achieve 269.5 points and not pass. That score is not rounded up.

Regrettably, this first attempt was met with a negative result. I scored 251.50 with this effort. While I did not pass, I got so close to my objective. Because of how close I was, along with the fact that I could take a bar review course again free of charge, it was imperative I sit for the test again. I got too close to turn my back and close the door to my objective. My economic survival was at stake.

I sat for my second attempt in February of 1989. State bar exams are given twice a year – February and July. There was some lag time between taking the exam and being notified of the results. Fortunately, this attempt had a successful conclusion. When I received the notice, my name was included. I had passed on this second try.

It was exhilarating for me when I passed this test. After taking an oath, I would receive my license to practice. My dreams were coming true. With employment in the legal field as an attorney, I felt my struggles would lessen. Life would get easier. My next step would be to find gainful employment where I could put into practice the legal knowledge I had learned. Finally, I would begin to realize certain financial security.

I sent letters of application and résumés to offices in need of a new attorney like me. While I did receive some interviews, no job offer materialized. Like what my father did when he continued his effort to find employment with Marsh, I kept looking. It was at that time I experienced a life altering moment. I got called for an interview for a position with the Richland County Child Support Enforcement Agency in Mansfield, Ohio. This office had a staff attorney position available. After setting up a time, I left Columbus for the eighty-minute trip to Mansfield. While I was optimistic, I followed the words my father said to me: "Hope for the best, but expect the worst." Unfortunately, bad fortune accompanied me on that trip. I drove my 1975 Ford Mustang. However, the car started to have muffler problems. I really did not know if I could make it. To compound the problems, I had no idea how I would get it fixed or even be able to pay for it.

Whether the circumstances are good or bad, God does not discriminate in providing His blessings. The assistant director of this agency, Mary Ann Nore, interviewed me. The interview was very professional and affable. I even told her of the car problems I developed on the way to the interview. Upon hearing this, Ms. Nore offered me the position but also provided a little money to help me get back to Columbus. I cannot begin to convey my feelings when she hired me. I was comforted by her help as well. I was offered this position at $25,000 per year. At that moment, any anxiety about my financial survival quickly dissipated.

My life reached a pinnacle. However, that feeling was short-lived. I was scheduled to begin my first day on Monday, May 21, 1990. It was memorable because of the career step I was preparing to take. Unfortunately, that day is also remembered for adversity I experienced with my family.

My mother had health issues when she was in her youth. She had contracted rheumatic fever as a child. Significantly, this illness had affected a valve in her heart. Periodically, she would experience health problems because of this condition. The very day I started my new job, my mother suffered a minor stroke. I had a lot of mixed emotions during that time. I was excited to go down a more secure road in my life. However, I loved my mother. While she only had minimal damage, the stroke altered some of the feeling in one of her hands and affected her speech in a minor way. My heart truly ached for her.

However, just like my father when he continuously got ready and went to work at Marsh, I went to work at the Richland County Child Support Enforcement Agency. This work was confined to a certain area of the law: child support. As a result, I could focus my attention on gaining the expertise for this specialized position. While the position did have its stresses, these stresses were reduced because of the repetitive nature of the cases I was handling.

The summer of 1990 passed, as did the autumn months. I continued working and managed to stabilize my economic standing. My mother's condition improved. However, just like the rapid formation of a tornado, my life soon experienced a dramatic upheaval. There would be, cast over my mind and heart, a very ominous shadow with lasting ramifications.

It was Monday, December 10, 1990. I received a telephone message from my brother, John. John said he needed to talk to me about something important. He wanted me to call as soon as I received this message. When I called, my mother answered the phone. She had something incredibly sad to tell me. As my mother was an emotional person most of the time, I was surprised by the lack of emotion in her voice. I guess she was trying to keep both of us from getting too upset. She explained that they had found my father dead by the bed earlier in the evening. She informed me of what had happened during the day. For one hour my father had a blanket on him and appeared to be resting; another minute, he had some labored breathing. Later, when my brother checked on him, he was lifeless.

My initial reaction was common. I was in shock. How could my father, my hero, be gone? How could he be dead? Was this real, or was I imagining these facts? He was only fifty-two years old.

That tragedy was the worst one I ever experienced or imagined. The timing of his death also raised my eyebrows. My father provided encouragement to me. He provided guidance and discipline in my life. Most of all, he provided encouragement for me to undertake, accomplish, and succeed. He was my hero in every sense of the word.

Like I said earlier, God has reasons for why things happen the way they do and the time they occur. After my father's passing, I was never happy with my job in Ohio. The main force behind what I wanted to accomplish was gone. I could no longer provide for him the way he had provided for me.

I reached toward his family in Arkansas for support. Initially, various family members provided support for me to deal mentally with this tragedy. Upon reflection, I felt Arkansas might be the place I should relocate. A year after his death, I decided to resign from my Mansfield position and relocate to Arkansas.

This is an early example of how I was practicing law, and circumstances dictated that I leave. I believe I had very legitimate reasons for making my decision. My faith focused on survival. While my economic strife began anew, I could work, study, and always try to get a law license in Arkansas. As God continually fertilized my spiritual maturation during the years, only God's nurturing hand revealed the prudence and viability of this decision. As I still did not realize the spiritual significance of happenings in my life, God then directed me to where His mighty hand desired me to go.

CHAPTER 6

RELOCATION TO
REALIZE A DREAM

Relocation to Arkansas

The death of my father was a devastating blow mentally for me as well as my family. While he did have some character flaws, those flaws were far overshadowed by many positive traits. He was a hard worker and loving family man who was truly committed to making sure his family felt loved, safe, and provided for. Most of all, he wanted life to be better for us than the consistent struggles he faced.

His death remains a mystery to me. There was no indication that he had been seriously ill or in a life-threatening circumstance. Because of the circumstances surrounding his death, the county coroner conducted an autopsy. Nothing out of the ordinary appeared in his report. The death certificate listed the following: No anatomic cause found. Cause of death--- natural.

While my father was a diligent, hardworking man, his main struggle was alcohol. Even so, nothing in the autopsy reflected that alcohol had anything to do with his passing. I have my thoughts about what happened. My father had a history of alcohol driving offenses. He had recently received the return of his driver's license.

However, shortly thereafter, he found himself in more trouble and lost his license again. I believe this setback had been hard for him; likewise, with the feeling that he had helped me get to where I needed to be and was not needed, he simply lost the will to live.

Despite my hurt, I had to move forward. While I questioned God on why He allowed something like this to happen, I realized, that to preserve my mental well-being, I had to temper my grief and plan for the future. I continued to believe God had an interest in my economic survival and was looking after me. However, I was very naïve about the actual extent of His involvement in my life and heart.

My relocation to Arkansas was not only exciting but also induced pangs of trepidation. The trepidation rose from the circumstances and economic struggles I saw my Arkansas family had endured. To assist me, Grandma Tigue conveyed her feeling that it was acceptable for me to stay with her. My tentative plan was to prepare to sit for the Arkansas bar examination. The added benefit of being there was that I would be surrounded by family I thought would provide me with much-needed support and understanding. With four uncles and three aunts coupled with an almost limitless quantity of cousins, I had the opportunity to interact with many family members. To my father, spending time with his family was very important. While I focused on attaining my Arkansas law license, my family was a great source of strength. Since I was no longer alone for a significant length of time, they provided a distraction from my personal stress and the stress of my professional undertaking.

My first attempt to pass the Arkansas bar exam occurred in February 1992. To pass this three-day exam, a participant needed to have 75 percent correct. As with the Ohio exam, I failed in this effort. I was so close, for I only scored 74 percent right. The process of passing the Arkansas exam had many similarities with its Ohio counterpart. As mentioned, it was a three-day exam. I managed to get so close, it made me realize that, on the second try, I had to pass. Furthermore, I had come so far that giving up was not acceptable. My economic welfare was at stake. I also realized I was continually being prodded by an unseen force toward a certain direction at that time as I had been in all my youth and academic ventures. I had little reason to doubt that I would be able to receive my Arkansas law license with a little extra effort.

Sometimes when you think you are about to attain something that appeared unreachable, defeat seems to come out of nowhere to attempt to take you down. It is then that you really need to turn to God. Before I was scheduled to take the Arkansas bar exam the second time, another tragedy of considerable magnitude hit like the most devastating hurricane. In the evening before Easter (April 18, 1992), my mother died. On that Saturday, I received a phone call from my brother. He stated that our mother was in the hospital, suffering from double pneumonia. Additionally, he conveyed that the doctor was unsure whether she would make it. I immediately began the 740-mile journey at approximately 2:00 p.m. that afternoon. My journey began with a different car. When I was employed at the child support agency, I had managed to purchase a new Ford Escort GT. As I was driving, I made minimal stops to make haste to see my mother. However, something compelled me to look at the clock in my car. The time was 9:30 p.m. That was notable for what was to come.

I arrived in the wee hours of the morning (April 19). There was a light on in our living room. I knew something was amiss. My brother was typically in his bedroom at that time. As I walked in, my brother was sitting on a recliner in the living room. He told me our mother was gone. More importantly, she passed away at approximately 9:38 p.m. My most significant thought was that I did not make it in time to tell my mother how much I really loved her.

I was shocked and devastated by this news. My mother was only fifty-one years old. In approximately seventeen months, I lost the two most important people in my life. While I had realized my mother had been sick periodically in her life because of rheumatic fever, I really started to question God anew: Why my mother? Why so young? Why that time?

I still took the Arkansas bar exam in July of 1992. Although the attempt was mentally dampened by the disappointing news, I maintained focus. As the spirit to practice law diminished, I continued to be determined to reach the objective I had developed during my life. My parents would have wanted me to keep my head up and persevere.

The result felt anticlimactic. I succeeded on my second attempt. I received my Arkansas law license on August 26, 1992. While this moment was certainly exciting, I questioned where to go next. With the two most important people in my life gone, how would I manage without them?

Nevertheless, I had bills, so I decided to get a more menial job to tide me over. I began working for Kmart in Hot Springs. To digress for a moment, from the time I graduated high school, I have obtained a variety of work experience. Most of this experience was in retail. My first job was at the K-Mart store in Muncie, Indiana, in 1980. Unfortunately, both stores closed.

My enthusiasm to practice law continued; however, this enthusiasm diminished with the news of my mother. While I searched for legal positions, my focus became on developing my own solo law practice. When I was in Ohio, I studied a book on how to open and build your law practice. By establishing my own office, I would be my own boss. I would have no accountability other than to my clients, the judiciary, and the system I represented. The question was how I would get there.

Marriage

Even when you do not really ask, God will continue to provide what you need. I have said little on the subject of romance. As it was difficult for me to meet and interact with women, I usually utilized personal ads or dating services to establish dates. Also, many women in my life possessed less-than-enviable qualities that will be outlined later.

After my mother's death, I really needed someone in my life to fill the void of both parents. It was sometime after my mother's death that God answered this need.

Her name is Lisa Jackson. When we first started our dialogue in the fall of 1993, it was discovered she had many interests like me. She was also originally from Indiana. She and her family lived in Pleasant Grove, Arkansas. The distance was approximately a 120-mile drive from my grandmother's house, near Amity. From the moment we met, our relationship seemed to click. We began to spend a great deal of time together and yearned for even more. While we spent time watching movies or traveling, we both had the sentiment that we should make our relationship more permanent. Late in 1993, I managed to pop the question. On April 30, 1994, Lisa and I were married. At the time, it was one of the most important moments in my life. A constant companion beside me would help me achieve again after overcoming the tragedies that I had experienced. After marriage, we would finally seek to establish roots in Pleasant Grove after living in Hot Springs and with her grandfather in Florence, Alabama.

Photo of Darrell King and Me (Wedding, 1994)

This photo of Darrell and me was taken the day before my first wedding to Lisa Jackson on April 29, 1994. Darrell has been a great friend for over forty years and lived at the beginning of our tiny lane. This photo was taken at the Pleasant Grove (Arkansas) Missionary Baptist Church in Pleasant Grove, Arkansas

Photo of Darrell King and Me (Wedding Day, 1994)

This second photo of Darrell and me was taken the
day of my wedding to Lisa on April 30, 1994.

Although I had my law license, I began working third shift
at the Walmart store about twenty-five miles away in Batesville to
help with our bills. Lisa also worked mainly at a small family type
convenience store in Pleasant Grove operated by her father. Although
the jobs helped us manage, my heart began to focus intensely on
returning to practice law. I studied a lot of basic legal information
on our computer. I wanted to keep current on all legal developments
in Arkansas. While I did not actively seek employment with a law
office, I began to realize that when the timing was ripe, I would
manage to open my own law office. I even participated in at least one
case involving a cousin I had near Amity.

Throughout life, God will manage to blindside believers with
blessings they never would have fathomed. One must be patient and
make no demands. That is what happened to me in the spring of

1998. Lisa understood my desire to want to practice law again. One day, she came into the room as I was studying and asked me if I wanted to go to Mountain View. She inquired if I was interested in looking for space for me to open a law office.

As there was little doubt what my answer would be, we ventured the fifteen-mile trek to Mountain View. We looked at two different locations. The first space we encountered was a spacious house. That was definitely too big for my purpose. I was just one attorney in need of space for me and maybe a secretary/receptionist. Moreover, the size of that office would be cost-prohibitive. The second possibility was more favorable. The office used to be a real estate office. Additionally, it was situated diagonally opposite the Stone County Courthouse. When you entered, there was a reception/greeting area with space for a secretary and desk. Through a door in the back and to the left, there was a very small office for me, a computer, printer, and desk as well as chairs for clients. It was as if God created this little office space for me.

I asked Lisa, "How can we afford to undertake an objective this great?" She simply told me she and I would ask my father-in-law, Dan Jackson, for a loan to open my practice. Any ominous clouds remaining from my past quickly dissipated.

That evening, Lisa and I visited her father. We told him what we did that day. We explained our proposition: we needed a loan to open a law office. I also explained my work ethic, how I was still employed at Walmart, and how, without question, I would liquidate any loan he would provide. It seemed as though a dream that had always been so far away was now so close, I could reach out and touch it.

With a stern but fatherly voice, he stated that he was willing to provide the loan. He lent us a mere one thousand dollars, but that was enough for me to get started. He dictated what the terms would be. They were fair and generous. All my struggles for security and economic survival seemed to once again to be nearing their end.

On April 20, 1998, I opened my office. It was the most incredible blessing experienced. My first client was an elderly woman desiring a divorce. I stated my fee, we agreed on terms, and I embarked on her representation.

In my life, I have struggled greatly at times. God was with me during those instances. Even during the gloomy times, God intervened to lift me and continue me down the path He wanted me to go. Likewise, I have had many blessings like graduating high school, college, and law school along with receiving my law licenses. Finally, He blessed me with the ability to practice law in my own law office. Sometimes, I even wonder how I am able to experience the things I have in my life. Despite the good times I embarked on that April, it never occurred to me that God had even better plans but would not want me to practice law for any extended time.

CHAPTER 7

THE LORD GIVETH,
THE LORD TAKETH AWAY

In April 1998, I began a venture I never expected. In addition to questioning why the tragedy of losing my parents occurred, I questioned why God allowed me on this path of operating my own law office. I started to develop a clear understanding that I was not living my life alone. However, I still did not comprehend how to really interact with God.

While my focus remained on finances and getting ahead, I was marching further down the path God was laying for me. My faith was starting to branch out from more than praying for economic survival. As times started to get better than I had experienced, I was drifting toward God's love. There was a mutual love that would start to permeate very slowly into every aspect of my life.

Since my boyhood years, this time had to be the best time I had ever experienced. When I was not in my office, I would be with Lisa. Lisa and I had the enviable opportunity of traveling a great deal together. Moreover, she provided me with the necessary company by filling the huge void the deaths of my parents had left.

With my relentless work ethic inherited from my father, I began working at my law office daily. As a general practitioner, I took on any legal matter I felt I was competent to handle. I always had a concern in my mind I might do something to malpractice. Nevertheless, I handled matters from divorces to minor criminal cases to drafting wills, deeds, and other contracts.

My interaction with the judges and my colleagues enhanced my effectiveness as a solo practitioner. Prior to my opening my law office, I attended court proceedings regularly to get a personal glimpse of the judges, other attorneys, and how they operated. These court proceedings included municipal court matters, chancery court matters, and finally circuit court matters. Each type of court handled its own type of legal considerations. As a result of this interaction with the various courts, God blessed me with a number of successful cases during my tenure as a solo practitioner. There was one case in particular that was worthy of noting here. It involved a male client who had joint custody of his nine-year-old daughter. The mother wanted their daughter to move with her and her live-in boyfriend. On a Monday morning in September 1999, the father came into my office. He was distraught since the mother took the child from school in Mountain View. She also had the child enrolled in the Timbo schools (thirteen miles away) that same day. This action clearly affected their joint custody arrangement. The father wanted to know what I could do to help him in returning his daughter to Mountain View.

Until that moment, most of my cases did not have a significant degree of complexity. The course of action in this particular matter would require delicate thought. After a moment of reflection, I finally arrived with a legal means in which to assist my client. I drafted a petition for a temporary restraining order. After advising my client of my proposed action, I prepared the necessary pleading along with an order that needed to be signed by a judge. Upon drafting and filing this petition, I decided to call the particular judge in this matter--- the Honorable Judge John Norman Harkey. I wanted to fill him in on the action I was taking and that it was imperative that the child be returned to Mountain View. She was well adjusted and excelled academically there, had many friends at school, and it would not be in her best interest to be uprooted to Timbo, circumventing the joint custody agreement and her welfare.

To digress momentarily, one of the first judges I personally met in my initial courtroom observations was Judge Harkey. While he was an older and very old-fashioned jurist, he had a very personable and affable quality that outweighed any gruffness in tone. After my call to him, he invited me to come to his office in Batesville so he could review the petition. This meeting exceeded any expectations I could have predicted.

When I arrived, I provided my petition along with an order I desired signed when appropriate. As I explained the facts, Judge Harkey was sifting through my petition; however, it was clear he was not reading the words verbatim. I also submitted my prepared order. He briefly reviewed this order as well. After providing the facts, he surprisingly took my order and signed it with no further explanation. Generally, orders of this nature are not signed *ex parte* (i.e., without the opportunity to be heard from the opposing party). In my mind, I was shocked at what had transpired. With this order in hand, I could present the filed copy to my client so he could proceed with a deputy to get his daughter returned to Mountain View. To date, that had to be the most significant accomplishment in my legal career.

Moreover, there was another career development that was not expected but worthy of note. Another judge I was acquainted with presided over the municipal court--Judge Nevada Richardson. Like Judge Harkey, she was older, old fashioned, and gruff in tone and demeanor. However, she too was one of the most personable individuals you could ever meet. I could not have picked a more appropriate mentor in the judiciary.

Unfortunately, sad news seemingly blindsided me occasionally during my life. This news has led to eventual unforeseen blessings. One day, as I was filing some paperwork with the municipal court clerk, I was informed that Judge Richardson had unexpectedly passed away. It was an understatement to say that my colleagues, family, and I were saddened and in shock. Despite the suddenness, Lisa told me that they needed to fill this vacancy until a special election. As a result, Lisa and some family and friends prodded me to put my name in the running for that judicial appointment. At that moment, I was apprehensive whether I had the prerequisite experience. However, I ultimately decided to be considered to fill this untimely vacancy. Consequently, here is what happened. I was working in my office one morning in 1999. My office phone rang, and I answered it like I did every other call, "Law office". On the other end, a gentleman commented it was Governor Huckabee's office calling. (Mike Huckabee was the governor of Arkansas at the time.). He informed me his office wanted me to fill the vacancy until a special election could be held. To say I was in shock was such a gross understatement.

I never thought I would ever be a judge. It was enough for me that I was practicing law. I was getting more blessings at that time than I could imagine. First, I had a law office. I had several successful cases. On top of everything, I received the call to be a judge. If it were not clear before, I was beginning to realize God was having even more of an influence in my life and career.

Sadly, there is a phrase, "All good things must come to an end." After the turn of the century, my life took even bigger turns than I could anticipate. God provided me a taste of what success I could have as a lawyer. However, as I was firmly mindful of His existence, He had other plans for me. Nothing could shake my belief in His very presence. After the beginning of the year 2000, Lisa had begun to experience some health issues. I initially thought she had just developed stomach problems. However, the problem was much deeper than that. Her health then dictated the course of my life. I would leave my law practice without knowing if I would ever have that opportunity to practice again.

Lisa had developed an eating disorder---classic anorexia/bulimia. Unfortunately, she also had other addictive problems. She was an alcoholic. While she was in the hospital, getting her gall bladder removed, she developed an addiction to pain killers. Like my father, I saw her in conditions another person should not see in someone they genuinely cared about. Like with my mother, my heart truly ached for her.

As the stress of this illness was enormous, I made the decision to close my law office. While I thought I wanted to help Lisa regain her health, the main reason for the office closure was because I could no longer do a satisfactory job for my clients. Despite my decision, I hoped I would eventually be able to practice law again.

Early in my life, God planted seeds of blessings He could provide if only I was receptive to them. At first, the focus was praying for economic survival. He wanted me to learn about Him through my early years and my education. He wanted me to perceive that life's blessings included more than mere economic welfare. However, the intensity really started to rise when He blessed me with my law office. Now He saw that my economic security was taken away. His most important objective was whether I would continue to rely on Him in spite of the giving and then taking away of a dream. He truly wanted me to love Him. My commitment remained steadfast in the direction He wanted me to go.

CHAPTER 8

STRUGGLES TO FIND
GOD'S REAL PATH:
THE JOURNEY STARTS

Second Marriage

When I was born, God began creating a path for which His hand would guide me. I struggled, but He was there to calm the stress in those times. When I had achieved, His hand was there to nudge me back on His divine path. When I closed my law office, I thought God would provide the route for my eventual return to law. However, like a shepherd prodding his sheep, God was taking me in a more divine direction to an even greater objective: the meaning of love.

When Lisa first became ill, we had been married for over six years. There was absolutely no forewarning of her condition. She had been instrumental in helping me fulfill the dream of opening my law office. We had traveled a great deal and were seemingly enjoying life. As Lisa's condition grew more pronounced, I did what a faithful and loving husband would do. I supported her and was hopeful for a full recovery. After closing my office, I once again drew on my retail experience. I returned to my overnight job at Walmart in Batesville to make ends meet.

I visited Lisa frequently in her hospital stays. I tried to support and encourage her the best way I knew. However, the nature of her addictions truly got a very unpleasant hold on her. Because of her eating disorder, she lost a significant amount of weight in a very short length of time. I was beginning to feel it was beyond my ability to assist her.

Like with my father, addiction is a tough condition for loved ones to observe. I began to feel that I was helpless to do anything to steer her to a complete recovery. In the back of my mind, my thought was that there would always be a threat of relapse, even if her health improved. Why I did not fully turn to God then, I do not know the answer. Even with attempts to reconcile, I felt it prudent that Lisa and I divorce.

When Lisa and I separated and eventually divorced in 2003, my economic struggles were once again inevitable. However, my employment at Walmart was helping to alleviate a significant amount of stress. However, the emptiness that I felt upon my parents' death returned with even sharper pain. I felt it imperative to try to find someone to help fill this reopened wound.

Love is a strange and intangible emotion. When someone feels like this person has found love, this emotion can disguise itself in a variety of alternative emotions. For example, one can think they are in love, but actually develop an emotional and financial dependence on that person. I believe that kind of love is what existed between Lisa and me. With Lisa contributing financially, I relied on her a great deal for support, especially when there was lesser demand for my legal services.

During our separation leading to the divorce, my life began to take a series of twists and turns. I tried dating to a significant degree. Basically, although I was looking for love, I never seemed to find it in its true form. Additionally, with my compassionate and caring personality, it opened my heart to a certain gullibility. I seemed to cater to the needs of the women I started to date. For the most part, I gave little thought to myself.

These relationships dictated that I move frequently. I relocated from Batesville to Harrison to be near a woman I started a relationship with. She was older than me and had a charismatic and enticing personality that revealed a vulnerability I had. The loss of my parents left my heart susceptible to retaining an emotional dependence on a calculating woman like her. What I thought was love was the cunning manipulation of someone who knew how to exploit this vulnerability. I would give more of myself, especially financially, before thinking about me.

During this time, I kept in contact with my brother who relocated to Kentucky after our mother's passing. While he did not make demands or his opinions explicit, I knew he was troubled that I did not fully focus on career but pursued women. He wanted me to find myself before any romantic involvement. However, I did not seem to want to hear what he was trying to tell me.

I continued to search to try to locate my one true love. Once found, I thought I would be able to focus more clearly on my career in law along with securing my financial stability. This strategy seemed to be contrary to what wisdom dictated. Additionally, there was a lot of instability in my romantic life. After I saw how calculating the Harrison woman was, I continued searching with the result being to jump into each relationship that passed before me.

I suppose I thought I would find someone, like Lisa, who would assist me in attaining my goals. As my search continued, I eventually moved from Harrison to Fayetteville. After some time working at a Fayetteville Walmart, I finally met someone I felt would fill the void my parents had left. Moreover, I felt this relationship would provide the stability needed to resume my law practice.

Her name is Jacqueline. At first glance, she was as pretty and sweet as anyone I had ever met. Like Lisa, we clicked and seemed to be on a path to a loving and lasting relationship. It was in November 2007 when Jacqueline and I got married after a brief romance. While this relationship was problematic from its inception, Jacqueline and I made every attempt to work through any adversity.

I continued working at Walmart. However, after a few employment opportunities, Jacqueline found herself unemployed. While I have an old-fashioned mentality and believed she did not have to work if she did not want to, the economic climate existing then necessitated that it was easier when both the husband and the wife were working.

What made our relationship problematic was that Jacqueline had serious anxiety issues. A part of her anxiety was the result of believing I was seeing or longing for other women. I tried to assure her that infidelity was not an issue in our marriage. I just had typical feelings (e.g., when a woman passed in a bikini, what men would not turn their heads?). While that seemed simplistic, Jacqueline felt a lot of anxiety even with the appearance of me merely looking at or watching another woman wherever she was (even on television). On the other hand, while working third shift at Walmart, I always called her on breaks and visited her for lunch. My inquiry toward her was how I would even have an opportunity to cheat.

Despite these problems for which we sought counseling, one spring day in 2010, I went to Jacqueline with a significant proposition. Jacqueline wore hearing aids, so she could pursue higher education at no cost to her. At that time, I had also been at Walmart from 2002 to 2010. My suggestion had two prongs: one, she should pursue her education; and two, I would give Walmart my two-week notice, get my accumulated 401(k)/profit sharing amount, and make a down payment on a law office. It would be a bold endeavor on our parts. Jacqueline had already enrolled in a truck driving course at Springdale Technical Institute. Since her father was a truck driver, Jacqueline wanted to get her CDL (commercial driver's license). Her goal was to seek employment as a truck driver for one of the local corporations, possibly Tyson.

We agreed to the terms. However, while we seem to have carefully thought out this course of action, God intervened with

His response. After one day of training in a classroom full of men, anxiety grabbed Jacqueline by the hand and pulled her away from the class. After one day in May 2010, she never went back. Because of this occurrence, my life was really placed in a perilous position. Not only was Jacqueline without a possible opportunity, but the funds from Walmart would also need to be utilized for our very survival. We were both without any significant employment prospect. It was at that moment I really began to feel God was my only hope--my divine answer.

With this turn of events, my marriage was under more stress than at any time. My economic survival was brought to the fore. As God was the only strength I could rely on, I asked Him for His divine assistance. It was then that I really made the effort to start praying.

This stress took a destructive toll on my marriage to Jacqueline. With her anxiety, now coupled with loss of employment prospects, the situation created irreparable damage. Finances were running out, and I had little encouragement, especially since I left Walmart. This stress would lead to an inescapable decision. One day in the summer of 2010, I had Jacqueline sit down so we could talk. I explained our troublesome marriage. I discussed her anxiety about me. I told her there was only one inevitable decision to preserve our very existence. We needed to divorce. As that already happened once with me, it was difficult to plan to go that route again.

Unbeknownst to me, that discussion would have a detrimental consequence. As I was attempting to establish interviews and find eventual employment, it was important that I had the ability to get to the appropriate location. One day, when Jacqueline returned, I asked her to borrow the car. She informed me that she sold it. Once she informed me that the car was gone, it was as if someone hit my legs with a sledgehammer. Any interviews would be difficult to attend because I would have to struggle to find a way. While there was a city bus system, my finances were running out. I had to be very diplomatic with any expenditures I encountered.

I no longer had a source of economic support. My next attempt at opening a law office was met with an unexpected turn of events. It was hard not to get discouraged. Fortunately, my faith and eventual love for God would slowly begin to get stronger.

God had firmly put His hand in mine. He wanted me to put all my faith in Him. Once done, this faith would reveal how God really wanted me to find that true love I had been missing in my life. My continued relationship with Jacqueline was not the true love I thought I had found. The feeling was a pity for her because I felt she had no other place to go. Despite this adversity, I began walking the long path to find my true love to fill the void in my life: the path to God's divine love.

CHAPTER 9

STRUGGLES TO FIND GOD'S REAL PATH: THE JOURNEY CONTINUES

Wandering Alone---Fayetteville, Truck Driving, God Talking to Me

Faith followed me from the moment I was born. Faith can be defined as the complete trust and confidence in God. However, this faith started out weak early on but only grew stronger with time. My belief was steadfast that God was watching over me. God only wanted me to understand that the power of faith would open the doors for many blessings for me.

The need for faith was more pronounced during the ordeal I found myself facing toward the end of my second marriage. This faith eventually opened my eyes to the biggest understanding I could ever discover. God kept me on His path. More importantly, He led me directly to the paramount revelation: the presence and significance of His divine love.

I had to maintain my focus and persistence. I needed employment to survive. I needed to discern the best way to achieve that. Without a vehicle, this effort was as challenging as any obstacle

I had ever encountered. Many thoughts began running through my head. As employment at Walmart had provided significant financial security through the years, I no longer had that as an option. I also did not want to return to those third-shift stocker days. I had to develop other options.

When considering possibilities, I also considered I no longer had a vehicle. Most of my efforts would need to be undertaken on foot. Hence, I began walking on a bike path three miles, one way to the Fayetteville Public Library, to begin my employment efforts. My thought was that I would utilize their computer in a valiant attempt to find a job.

While I perused employment possibilities online, there seemed to be something specific I was looking for. I had to find a position that addressed my lack of transportation. Furthermore, I had to find employment that met or exceeded the financial obligations I had. It seemed to be an almost impossible quest.

During my walks along the bike path, I started talking to God. I conveyed to Him that my life was in His hands. I placed my heart and well-being in His arms. I wanted to completely surrender to Him. I prayed God would take me to where He wanted me to go. Finally, I accepted the direction He was leading me.

While continuing my trips to the library, God revealed a possibility to me. I asked myself, "What is the best way to get training quickly with little or no expense, leading to a job where you can reimburse the cost of the education while working?" My past revealed a lot of answers to questions such as these. I thought to myself, why not attend truck driver training school and obtain a CDL? Once again God helped me formulate an answer to a seemingly impossible question. I began attending a truck driving school in North Little Rock. One day, as I walked around a semi, I asked myself, "Are you really going to drive this big rig?" I had never thought this experience would even remotely be a possibility.

After about a month of training, I managed to pass the test requirements for a CDL. I received a job offer from PAM Transport

Services, Inc. based in Tontitown, Arkansas. Soon, I was assigned an experienced driver trainer. This driver trainer taught me and provided his expertise at the early stage of my driving career. As a result, I would begin a short-lived experience of driving an 18-wheeler.

Even though my driving experience was short-lived, it was during the driver training that I had an experience that profoundly impacted my faith. My driver trainer and I had the opportunity to venture out west to pick up and deliver a few loads. We traveled through many western states, including California and Oregon. More importantly, we traversed through the freeway in Oregon by the Columbia River Gorge. We could see the state of Washington on the other side of the river. This was one of the most beautiful areas I had ever seen.

While traveling through Oregon, I began to sense something I had never experienced before. This sensation became even more pronounced during my excursion through part of the hills near San Bernardino, California. I felt like someone was trying to communicate with me. However, I could not make out what was being said. In my heart, I believe God was attempting to communicate with me.

As I could not interpret what was being conveyed, I knew vividly what sensation I was experiencing. Although there were no words, I knew God was trying subtly to interact with me. I even prayed He would be clearer in this contact. Like the wind blowing through my hair, I knew the sensation was there, even though I could not actually see or hear anything.

Unfortunately, my career as a truck driver was short. Because of some safety issues, I was terminated from my position. It was long enough, however, that God made clear He was continuing to direct me. I needed to continue traversing this path. However, once again my economic welfare catapulted to the fore. While the stress started anew, my faith helped to alleviate some of the emotion. As I had little money nor options, I knew I had to leave my apartment in Fayetteville. I had a female friend (Michelle) who was willing to take me in with her two sons. She lived in Bentonville and worked as a nurse. The main benefit of maturing is that you begin to learn from your past. While Michelle wanted a serious romance, my focus was on establishing myself and getting my finances in order. I rebuffed her attempts at establishing a serious commitment. My most important objective was becoming independent, getting on my own two feet, and finally resuming a law practice.

Regrettably, another twist in my life was on the horizon. While I was living with Michelle and she was providing financial security, food, and shelter, I continued to have difficulty finding employment. Almost daily I would utilize her computer. I would frequently look at employment opportunities with the purpose of obtaining an interview. The attempts met with little success. These efforts continued for some time; however, they ended abruptly when Michelle decided to relocate to Tulsa, Oklahoma. She did not give any indication to me she would be moving. On a muggy day in July 2011, I was watching the Casey Anthony trial unfold on Court TV. I heard a knock on the door to the house Michelle was renting to own near Gentry, Arkansas. It was the landlord of the premises. The landlord conveyed to me that Michelle was behind on her rent. He dictated that if a significant payment was not forthcoming, Michelle would be evicted by the end of the week. Upon hearing this, I voiced my concern about what would happen to me. He clearly stated that I would have to go too.

While both my concerns and stresses were high, my faith remained unwavering. I contacted only one person I thought may be able to assist me: Barbara Janelle Tigue. Janelle was a first cousin and the daughter of my Uncle Ed. She made it clear that I could stay with her family (husband Bob and a teenage son, Brandon) until I managed to stand on my feet. Grandma Tigue had passed away years earlier, so I did not have the option of staying with her. God was directing me down the final leg to the most important objective he had for me: His divine love.

Without a vehicle, I had to make plans on how to journey from near Gentry to Hot Springs. First, I had to get to the bus station in

Fayetteville. From there, I would ride a bus to Hot Springs where Bob would be waiting to pick me up and drive me the rest of the way to Amity. My only option was to start the trek by walking from near Gentry to Fayetteville.

On a hot Wednesday morning, I began my journey on foot. The distance from Gentry to Fayetteville is over thirty miles. As I never like to impose on anyone, my intention was to walk all day to see how far I could get. As a necessity, Michelle allowed me to pawn some items for money for a bus ticket and any other pertinent need I might develop. I planned to stay at a motel if I could not make the entire distance that day.

With only thirty dollars to my name along with a black-and-red duffle bag I purchased from Walmart containing my meager belongings, I began walking down the dirt road toward Fayetteville. I had no idea what was going to happen to me. Did my future entail an opportunity to ever practice law again? I had time to think about these issues during my journey.

I have endured many struggles and hardships during my life. On the other hand, I have had successes from which I have found great security and comfort. However, the journey I was set to embark on would be the most important time of my entire life. Its end would finally reveal the path God was taking me on and its ultimate divine purpose. While apprehensive about leaving Gentry, I was excited since faith was taking me to where I needed to be. I was about to even realize the objective for which God had wanted me to reach with all the events occurring in my life: my financial security and true love.

CHAPTER 10

STRUGGLES TO FIND GOD'S REAL PATH: THE JOURNEY REVEALS THE PATH

Rescued by God

Since my birth, God has taken me on a journey from which He wanted me to learn about Him. First, He wanted me to know He was there, that His existence was clear. In time, He wanted me to know He would provide for my needs as long as I believed. He would alleviate any financial insecurity through blessings and the support of my family and friends. Secondly, He wanted me to develop a strong faith in Him, no matter what happened, He would provide the path for blessings when they were needed. Finally, He wanted me to genuinely love His spirit.

My trip from Gentry to Hot Springs was a continuation of this journey. As I was walking in the hot sun toward Fayetteville, I prayed that God would make His presence felt. I prayed He would keep me safe and out of harm's way. I had no doubt He heard and watched over me.

My objective was to get to Fayetteville. God must have sensed the immediacy of my need. After walking about a mile, a white truck pulled up next to me. This little act provided a significant blessing for me to get to my destination.

The driver was a young man. I guess he was in his early twenties. He inquired if I needed any assistance. I explained to him my situation. While he indicated that he might only be able to take me to Springdale (just north of Fayetteville), that gesture was a tremendous help in getting me closer to the bus station. I got in, and he told me his name was Chris. During our trip, he stated he was heading to work. He checked with his boss to see if he could take me the entire distance to Fayetteville. Once in Springdale, his boss assented to the trek. There is little question that my reliance completely on faith had provided this blessing for me.

Once in Fayetteville, I was able to visit a pawn shop, arrive at the bus depot, and begin the bus ride to Hot Springs. Janelle's husband, Bob, picked me up once I arrived in Hot Springs. It was getting late in the evening. As we drove out of Hot Springs, Bob made a suggestion that proved to be another significant blessing.

Burger King

Bob understood my need for work. We were getting close to a Burger King that had just opened. He asked me if I would be interested in stopping to fill out an employment application. As I had been unemployed since my truck driving experience, it was clear what my answer would be.

Once at Burger King, I went in and asked for an application. Once completed, I gave it to an associate and asked to speak to the manager. Unfortunately, I was informed that the manager would not be available until the next morning. I left my application with the comment that I would call about a job. The following morning, I called and was able to speak to the manager. He invited me to come in for an interview. During the interview, he expressed his apprehension as to why a lawyer would want to work at Burger King. My simple retort was, because of my circumstances, I had an immediate need for any type of work. I thought of the efforts of my father when I made this statement. While the manager continued to manifest his apprehension, he conveyed that the store needed a broiler operator. He was willing to take a chance on me. While the job was part time (twenty hours) and close to minimum wage ($7.35 per hour), I was willing to take the job. My belief was that God would make a blossoming flower out of the planting of a little seed.

I mentioned these specifics for a divine reason. I was ecstatic about drifting into this new job. At that moment, I felt God was blessing me with what He felt I needed. Most importantly, I do not believe things are coincidences. I believe God has a hand in everything. This was clear when I heard the manager's name: Chris. After that, there was no doubt in my mind God has been and will always be watching over me.

While I stayed with Janelle and Bob, the question was how I would be able to get back and forth to work. Bob worked at an O'Reilly Auto Parts store just down the street from Burger King. Even though our shifts did not really overlap, I had transportation with Bob to get back and forth to work. I sometimes had to wait an inordinate amount of time before or after my shift. Nevertheless, I was willing to do what was necessary to work and bolster my finances.

I started this position on July 7, 2011. The arrangements we developed continued throughout the year. Unfortunately, an event transpired which uprooted my life again. Although Janelle's attitude might have been the result of life's stresses, she implicitly indicated that she no longer wanted me living with her. On New Year's Eve, I moved to Hot Springs.

Prayer in Hot Springs and the Wording of Prayer

My move to Hot Springs started a new chapter in my life. I eventually managed to find a room at a motel on Ouachita Avenue. It was like an efficiency apartment that I rented by the week. The motel was two miles from Burger King. As I still had no vehicle, my job was close enough to be within walking distance.

Whenever I was scheduled, I would begin the hike to get to work. Regardless of the weather, I would traverse the distance to Burger King and return to my apartment. However, when the weather turned unpleasant on limited occasions, some of my Burger King co-workers would offer me rides. For the most part, however, many days were spent walking to that Burger King and returning to my room.

I maintained the thought that I wanted to return to practicing law. I possessed some bar review material I consistently reviewed to help me retain my legal knowledge. Furthermore, I also had a little cell phone that allowed me to access legal material online. I even asked God to bless me with attaining that goal when He felt the time was right.

Because of struggles throughout my life, I became very frugal in managing finances. I only spent money on essentials along with what I felt I needed. Because of that mentality, I managed to save quite a bit even when working part time at minimum wage for an establishment like Burger King. It was that effort that eventually paid off in a big way during this time and even later in my life.

As I started to tire from the wear the continual walking had on my body, I renewed my prayer to God: "How long will I have to continue walking and working at Burger King? Will I be able to practice law again? If so, when?" Finally, I expressed a bit of sentimentality when I asked God, "When will I return to Indiana to see my brother and my best friend, Darrell?" I had not seen my brother (who had relocated to Winchester, Indiana) or Darrell (who settled in Anderson many years prior) for several years. God always hears prayers, yet He will answer them in His time and often in extraordinary ways.

While the parental void continued in my heart, I often found women to date. By that time, Jacqueline and I had divorced. However, many women lacked the qualities I felt were prudent to pursue. Hence, any relationship developing then was for a brief moment. They were short until I finally met an extraordinary woman. It was my desire to have a relationship with her that created the events that led me to the realization of the path God had me wander on all along.

Her name is Isabella, but she preferred Bella for short. She was a classy stereotype of a Southern belle. She was short, petite, sweet, and very pretty. My heart raced in her presence. She was an ideal dream girl that men often fantasize about meeting and getting to know. I longed to have a long-term relationship with Bella. For the romance with Bella to occur, I knew my experience at Burger King eventually had to come to a close. I knew I had to establish myself to be able to romance a beautiful and sophisticated woman like Bella. I would slowly begin to devise a plan I would set in motion. It would be that plan that would lead to my discovery of God's path and purpose.

Tripped by God's Littlest Messenger---God's Profound Answer

While I was working at Burger King, I did not own a vehicle. The first part of my plan was to look, find, and purchase a good used vehicle. A vehicle would provide the capability to visit Bella where she lived (near Conway, Arkansas). The second part of my plan was to look into the opening of my law office in Hot Springs. Through working at Burger King and with my frugality, I had saved four thousand dollars to allow me to pursue these goals. God had, in fact, made a blossoming flower from a meager seed.

Unfortunately, God had different plans for me. On the morning of September 3, 2013, I made a short walk to the bank to withdraw the weekly cost of my rent. When I was returning to the parking lot where I stayed, I told the manager to my left that I was going to pay my rent. She was getting into her vehicle. She replied that she had an errand to run but would return shortly. It was at that moment God sent His littlest messenger to visit me. I had little time to react. I was walking in midstride when I looked down. Underneath my right foot, there was a small dog lodged there. He was no more than a few feet lengthwise but very sturdy. Fearing that I would hurt its little back, I did not put all my weight down and managed to trip over it. Afterward, I felt I merely sprained my foot. Playing basketball as a kid, I had experienced many sprained ankles. Nonetheless, I should have known this injury was different. As I was trying to navigate the stairs where I lived, I could not place any weight on it. Later, a Burger King associate and good friend came by and observed this injury. Without hesitation, she said that I needed to visit the hospital emergency room. She was correct in her observation. While I denied that it was that serious, I indeed broke the fifth metatarsal bone in my right foot. The break also required surgery to insert a metal screw. This surgery was scheduled for September 11, 2013.

Once again, my law career would be placed on hold even before it got started. While my relationship with Bella fizzled, that divine intervention by that little pooch would open the door for the biggest love I could ever have imagined.

I returned to Indiana to live with my brother to recuperate. That unforeseen adversity finally revealed the path God had prodded me down in my life. It opened the door to the realization of how much God loved me and how much I began to love him. I finally found the true love that had eluded me throughout my life.

CHAPTER 11

THE PATH ENDS: REALIZING I HAVE FOUND TRUE LOVE

Where I Am and Where I Want to Be

Early in my life, I had a challenging, but simple goal to attain: to become an attorney. What should have been an uncomplicated journey was made very sophisticated by the will of God. He had provided a circular path for me so I could learn about Him. Most importantly, He wanted me to understand the realization that I had found the true love that I have yearned for in my entire life.

Through my experiences, I gradually understood the nature of God's presence. Although I had a thirst to regain my law practice, He was opening my eyes to His continual presence. I started to comprehend that little events happening in my life were blessings as a result of my faith. God was providing the spiritual sustenance I had relied on for my continued existence. What was not clear was the actual true love God had wanted me to finally perceive.

After I had the visit from God's littlest messenger, I was no longer able to work at Burger King. I needed a significant amount of time for my broken bone to heal. As a result of the surgery, I needed to develop another plan of action. I had some money saved, but I knew it would not last forever.

I no longer wanted to live in Hot Springs. To assist with my recovery, I asked Bella to help me in relocating closer to her near Conway. As I thought she had some feelings developing for me, she gave me the impression she would assist me any way she was able. After my surgery, I packed my things, and she drove me to a motel in Conway. I had limited funds for me to achieve my new objectives. Once at the Conway motel, I began looking for another place to reside. I was also looking for possible employment opportunities once my foot healed.

When Bella was not working, she was helping me deal with my physical inability along with finding me another home. Eventually, she saw an ad that was enlightening. There was a double-wide trailer for rent at an affordable cost that was closer to where she lived. Part of the trailer was rented by a prospective landlady's daughter and her husband. (The landlady was Melanie, and her daughter's name was Amanda. Amanda's husband was in the military stationed in Oklahoma City.) I would have the obligation of paying the other half of the rent. The cost was well within my budget.

I decided to move to this trailer located in Damascus, Arkansas. The understanding was that since Amanda's husband was in the military, Amanda and her husband would only be present there on rare occasions. However, because of marital circumstances, she spent much more time at the trailer than originally expected. As a result, I had the opportunity to get to know Amanda. While Amanda had a sweet demeanor, she also had a significant problem. Like my father and my two ex-wives, she was a serious alcoholic. Notwithstanding that issue, I developed a platonic connection with Amanda. Also, like my father, my heart ached for her addiction.

Sometimes one can confuse romantic love with dependence similar to what I experienced with my marriage to Lisa. Moreover, it can also be confused with a feeling of pity like I had when I did not leave Jacqueline immediately because of her anxiety. I initially felt that by separating, Jacqueline would have no place to go. Finally, feelings can appear as love, although in reality these feelings are caused by the mental manipulation exercised by the opposite sex as with the Harrison woman.

When I was living in Hot Springs, I began praying a lot. I already mentioned two prayer requests. The first was how long I would have to continue working at Burger King. I had the yearning to reopen a law office. The second question was when I would see my brother, John, and my best friend, Darrell, in Indiana. By sending His littlest messenger for me to trip over, God revealed the answers to both those prayers. However, there was a third and most important prayer request. I asked God the following, "When will I find that true love that had been elusive in my life? When will I find that true love to ultimately fill the void of losing my parents for which I had suffered with all my life?" Sometimes it is not what you pray for, but the words used in those prayers that meets with God's understanding. My request to find true love had been answered. However, it was not answered in the way I had anticipated, nor was it apparent until I returned to Indiana.

My feelings for Bella seemed strong. Bella, unfortunately, did not have these same feelings. This became obvious as my finances started to dwindle. Love had disguised itself as the financial manipulation of the opposite sex. Once I could no longer provide anything monetarily to our relationship, her time with me started to diminish. Eventually, I received a telephone call that Bella had gone to South Carolina. My heart was broken upon the news of Bella's travails. Once again, the void revealed with the death of my parents became obvious. However, the paramount struggle was to heal and find a way to survive financially. With Bella no longer helping me, this quest became more difficult. Furthermore, I had no close friends or family in the area that could offer me any form of crutch. Because of my circumstance, I began calling on God with more zeal and frequency. I asked Him in prayer to provide me comfort and to assist me. I was also impatient with the healing process for my foot. I almost climbed the walls because I wanted to work and provide an income for myself, no matter what opportunity appeared.

With my diminishing funds along with limited help, I was running out of options. However, the one option that God had kept visible remained: family. It was that connection to which I would rely on at this significant moment. I made the decision to call my brother, John.

After living many years in Kentucky, John had recently returned to Indiana. He had a daughter in Winchester whom he wanted to live closer to. He was managing financially as he was working for a Honda parts plant there. He extended the temporary invitation for me to live with him in Winchester until my foot healed and I returned to my feet. This offer was one of the most pertinent blessings I had in my life. I was blessed with a roof over my head. John provided me with the space needed for recovery. He also provided a location where I began my job pursuit anew. My familiarity with the area also worked to my advantage.

When I was in Damascus with Bella, I had also applied for food stamps and received a generous amount. It was hard for me to apply as I always had a high degree of pride. However, the circumstances warranted taking that step. I was in tears when I heard my application was approved. I maintained these benefits when I relocated to Winchester. Living with my brother, I could not begin to convey how crucial this benefit was to my livelihood. Such provision provided me with the bridge I needed to get to my first goal: becoming financially stable.

My life completely came to a full circle. I returned to the location where my life and my dreams had started. It was great to return home. Simple time spent with my brother, like walking back and forth to the neighborhood Village Pantry for cookies and coffee, was one of the highlights of my life. However, it was a meeting I later had with my best friend, Darrell, that provided the bright light on what God had wanted me to learn by living my life and the complex circular route it had taken.

I relocated to Winchester in early November 2013. Since I had not seen Darrell for a while, we talked via phone about meeting and spending some time together after I moved. The time was approaching the holidays, and I excitedly accepted this invitation. Because of not having my own car, he would have to drive to pick me up, drive to our destinations, and return to Winchester.

The holidays that year were very precious to me. Because of our indelible friendship, Darrell drove to Winchester to pick me up. We went near Selma to visit with his parents. I relived many memories of when I was just a young boy growing up. Through the years, I understood I had lived and learned. That journey was because of God's divine intervention and prodding hand. It was during this trip that God truly enlightened me with His purpose in taking me down the path He wanted me to go.

Darrell, his mother, and I went from Selma to Muncie to run an errand. On the return trip to Selma, reality hit me like nothing had hit me before. I can compare it to the feeling one gets when during a blizzard one opens the front door and feels the bitter, cold northwest wind hitting one's face. The answer had been obvious and in front of my eyes all along. I was making it far more difficult to understand than I should have. I had prayed for the answer on when I would experience the elusive true love I had never experienced in my life. Moreover, I needed to finally fill the void that vividly appeared with the death of my father and mother. God had, in fact, answered this prayer as He had with the other prayers I had requested when I lived in Hot Springs and thereafter. Simple reasoning revealed the divine solution. My law professors would be pleased with the development of my reasoning skills.

There is no doubt I have lived a tumultuous life. It is filled with excitement of my academic successes along with practicing law and even becoming a judge. Additionally, it is filled with the love and nurturing of great family and friends. Unfortunately, it has also been riddled with sadness---the death of my parents, the illnesses of my two ex-wives, closing my law office, and even the upheaval caused by tripping over God's littlest messenger. Yet the result of all these occurrences is the obvious love that through everything God will continue to provide the blessings necessary for my survival. This love was unconditional. As long as I believe and continue to believe in Him, He will take care of me in extraordinary ways. He will answer prayers and take me to where I need to go. Once I realized this during that simple trip, how can I not see God had indeed manifested in my heart, my mind, and my spirit the true love I desperately required during my life? In times of joy and sorrow, who will always be there for me? There would be no greater love I can ever find. It was that one trip, that one fleeting moment in time, that I realized God's true love had truly found me and my heart.

CHAPTER 12

LIVING GOD'S MISSION: TRAVELING GOD'S DIVINE PATH

Faith Will Direct Me to Where I Need to Go

God's true love had indeed found me. God had created the path that took me on a most unlikely and incredible journey. While I wanted to practice law, God had other plans for me. It was this divine purpose that far outweighed any security I could establish by practicing law.

From that moment, the void that existed because of the death of my parents was not as great as it had been. Although I loved and missed my parents deeply, my vision focused on what I needed to do to maintain my faith and God's blessings. Further, every fiber of my being was channeled toward what I needed to do to maintain this mutual loving relationship with God. God will always provide what I need now and in the future. I will never have to walk alone again.

When I first prayed that I would locate my true love, I was not specific in what I was asking from God. I never clarified I was searching for a true, worldly romantic love I had never experienced before. Because of this wording, God answered my prayer on His terms. He brought me an even greater gift: His divine and eternal love. Ultimately, He would be the pilot, directing me to where I needed to go in my life.

While living with John in Winchester, it did not take me very long to recuperate and reestablish myself. I had a little cell phone from which I completed my online employment applications. My foot had healed nicely. After the holidays, I was confident I would obtain employment. At that moment, God took any residual stress off my shoulders.

In January 2014, I completed an online application for my old employer: Walmart. I indicated I would accept employment at either one of the two Walmart stores in Muncie or the store in Winchester. Further, I continued lacking my own vehicle. Despite that issue, my faith reassured me that God would somehow bless me with what I needed to endure. Later that month, I was interviewed for a part-time job at Pizza Hut in Winchester. My phone began to vibrate in my pocket. Although the interview was pleasant, my preoccupation turned to that particular call. An associate from Walmart left a voicemail: Would I be interested in coming in for an interview?

My initial reaction was that the call was from the Winchester store. My assumption was incorrect. It was the Walmart store on the north side of Muncie (near Ball State University) that requested the interview. I had to develop a plan on how to get from Winchester to Muncie. Similar to the blessings I had encountered frequently during my life, God provided the answer. Winchester is located twenty-two miles from Muncie. Nonetheless, there is no barrier when God intervenes. While John had suggested he would help with a taxi, if necessary, it was a brief encounter that provided the answer. God sometimes answers prayers in most subtle ways.

About a month prior to the interview request, I was walking to the Winchester Walmart to obtain a prescription for my foot. At the traffic light immediately preceding the store, I was stopped by traffic. A car pulled up next to me. A woman named Kathy asked me if she could give me a lift. I explained I was just walking to Walmart. Despite the short distance, I accepted this ride.

Kathy went to church and was a devout Christian woman. She asked if I would be interested in coming to church with her sometime. I accepted since I felt that going to church would provide the feeling I was getting even closer to God.

While our contact was fleeting when I was in Winchester, I called her to help in my quest to get to Muncie. Although she was not available for the drive to my interview, she called a friend. This friend, Diane, gladly assisted me in getting to Muncie. God was prodding me down a path He wanted me to go.

Because of my experience, Walmart offered me a full time third shift position. Although the starting wage was close to the minimum wage, I excitedly accepted. Through Kathy's assistance, I succeeded in getting an apartment south of the Ball State campus along the bus lines. God was once again blessing me with His divine assistance.

Any anxiety concerning my financial security slowly dissipated. I now had a stable job with a stable income. Although I could take the bus to get back and forth to work, I remained within walking distance (3.13 miles) in case I had to make the trek by foot. I had a nice little apartment that was well suited for my needs. God had provided the path for my financial security.

In the back of my mind, I continued to have the desire to practice law. My new plan was to save money for the following: a computer, a car, and a fund to allow me to relocate to Arkansas and enroll in a bar review course. The purpose of the bar review was to refresh legal concepts in my mind before I would resume practicing. However, only God could determine the timing and extent I would reach these goals.

During the transition to my employment and apartment in Muncie, I had a trivial responsibility to address. I had to get my driver's license renewed even though I owned no vehicle. As I had an Arkansas license, its validity was about to expire. Hence, I needed to discern the steps needed to obtain an Indiana license.

Situations such as this truly opened my eyes to God and how He can delicately intervene in even the simplest circumstances with significant future consequences. I rode the bus close to a license branch in Muncie, then I walked the rest of the way. Upon arrival, a friendly worker informed me that I would need to take a knowledge test and a vision test. She gave relevant information to prepare for the knowledge test. I would need to study this material to better prepare me for this exam.

Thereafter, I began to prepare for this test. As with other obstacles, I would have little difficulty in passing the knowledge exam. Furthermore, as I recently renewed a prescription for eyeglasses, I had no doubt I would have the necessary vision to obtain my new Indiana license.

Several days after my initial visit to this license branch, I returned. As expected, I experienced no difficulty in passing the knowledge test. The vision test provided me with another example of God's power in my life. The result would have a bearing on the meaning of why I am where I am today.

After passing the knowledge test, I was told where to go to take the vision test. As I approached the counter, I was preparing to take my glasses out of my pocket to proceed with the exam. However, the woman associate asked me if I would like to try taking the test without my glasses first. Since I had nothing to lose, I decided quickly that I would make this attempt.

What happened with that vision test still surprises me today. Naturally, my thought was that as you progressively age, your eyesight correspondingly diminishes. Without glasses, I recited the letters with little difficulty. As with the exams to receive my law licenses, I was incredibly surprised and elated when the associate told me I passed. I would have no restrictions on my new Indiana driver's license. Unbeknownst to me at that time, this accomplishment would be another example of how God was interacting with me and prompting me to journey down His chosen path for me.

As the months passed by, I renewed another prayer to God. This time, I was specific in what I was asking Him for. I continued searching for the one true romantic love I lacked in my life. I wanted a steady companion to confide in and share interests. I wanted to find someone to laugh and cry with. I also added the following, "Please provide her for me if you feel I am worthy. If not, then I will accept that while continuing walking down the path You have made for me." My love for God was becoming resilient and enduring.

With no vehicle and my caution with spending money, I started to save a slowly blossoming fund for my future. I intermittently tried to date using an online dating site. However, I was not as serious about dating as I once was. I filled my time by working, then returning home and watching movies on my first flat-screen television that John had gratuitously purchased for me. My heart and soul remained with God and the direction He desired me to go.

From January 2014 to December 2015 my life was relatively uneventful. I continued working, saving, and enjoying little blessings that I experienced. My focus was on my future. However, at that moment, God decided to send an angel into my life to further direct my course toward my faith and love of God. Her name is Angel Elizabeth Howell. Words can never do this woman justice for the type of Christian she was. She was compassionate, sensitive, caring, and loving. She lived up to her name. She was an angel in every sense of the word sent by God. I started dating Angel late in 2015. However, our relationship almost had an abrupt end before it even started. She was diagnosed with cancer in December of that year. Because she did not want me involved in her health plight, she almost stopped seeing me before our relationship ever really started. During this time, Angel was experiencing intense stress, not knowing what her future held. Fortunately, after conveying her diagnosis and course of treatment, I tried to be as supportive and caring a friend as possible. Because of our developing dependency on each other, our relationship seemed to blossom. God truly blessed every moment we shared.

Angel lived with her mother north of Connersville, in Milton. I felt the most prudent course of action was to relocate to be closer to her. As I felt she did not really have a good friend to lean on, I had the willingness and desire to see her through this dark time. Moreover, I knew God had His reasons for crossing our paths.

Once again, circumstances led to a disruption of my life. However, I maintained my financial security merely by transferring to the Connersville Walmart. Any long-term plans were simply placed on hold. I had a new friend that needed my undivided attention during a most difficult time.

While my relationship with God was stronger than ever, I sought a lasting connection with Angel. In a short amount of time, I proposed marriage. Angel openly accepted. However, no tentative marriage date was set. For the brief time that I knew her, Angel and I spent a great deal of time together. We went to Metamora where we had the opportunity to partake in a romantic carriage ride. We dined out frequently after she left work. However, the most important memory was yet to come. She had always wanted to go to Memphis to see the mighty Mississippi River and visit Graceland.

Midway through 2016, Angel and I traveled to Memphis. We did, in fact, stand right next to the Mississippi River watching the barges pass. We also had a very enlightening tour of Graceland, the home of Elvis Presley. It was amazing what we saw and learned. Finally, we briefly drove by Beale Street, the home of the Blues. I know Angel appreciated every moment of this vacation. While I did not hear those exact words, I knew she felt indebted to me for assisting her in realizing a dream.

God had truly directed my life to the divine path He wanted me to travel. I had a decent job, a place to live, interests and, most importantly, a steady companion to get to know and spend time with. How could I not truly love God for the life I experienced, including the struggles and misfortune? I embarked further down God's path with my relationship with Angel. While Angel had a lasting impact in my life, the road God desired me to continue down surprisingly only included her in spirit.

The following poem was written prior to me ever meeting Angel Elizabeth Howell. Yet I feel as though God was commanding me to write this about her even before He would bring her into my life. I truly believe God was setting the stage for the future path I would journey with Angel. Finally, the poem's mention of "the hole in the wall" references the small efficiency apartment on Ouachita Avenue where I lived when I was in Hot Springs. God has truly entered my heart and has provided subtle blessings if only I was capable of seeing these wonderful things.

An Ode to An Angel

One evening as I lay down my head,
I dreamed a dream, a prayer to the Lord to be my guide.
A wish, a thought instead of sleep it led,
An intangible emotion I sought and could no longer hide.

The hole in the wall for which my existence would depend,
A change for the better and true love I would hope to find.
Something I never felt and for which my heart would yearn,
I prayed a prayer which I thought would only live in my mind.

Yet reality hit and I am still in a daze,
An Angel appeared to rid me of the haze.
Someone so incredibly unique,
It could only be the Lord sending her to speak.

As I got to know her, the commonalities abound,
A connection developed and a new feeling I had found.
A feeling of hope and encouragement grew,
I knew in my heart the Lord had sent my true love so I could really live
anew.

I escaped the hole in the wall with goals to attain,
With the Angel to guide me, to focus and rid my heart of its past stain.
With a vision of beauty to see and words from her lips to hear,
The path in my life had become ever so clear.

Now my hopes and aspirations are well within sight,
Guided by the Lord's blessings and His might.
Never to turn back to my old way of life,
I praise the Lord for the Angel in my sight.

No words of gratitude could ever convey,
The blessings of true love in my heart to stay.
Yet I thank you Lord for bringing her to me,
I will never forget my Angel and my heart will forever be free.

Frank D. Tigue
Copyright 9/29/2013

Photo of Angel and Me (New Year's Eve, 2015)

This photo of Angel Elizabeth Howell and me was taken December 31, 2015. I was just at the beginning stage of my relationship with Angel. While Angel and I only knew each other a short quantity of time, every moment was blessed with laughter and her compassionate nature. I truly believe she was an angel sent by God to reaffirm my love for Him and to learn how to treat others. Sadly, she succumbed to cancer on June 3, 2019. She will always live on in my heart and memory.

CHAPTER 13

LIVING GOD'S MISSION: WHERE GOD IS CURRENTLY TAKING ME

Through the years I have had little doubt in God's existence. Moreover, God had chosen the path my life had taken. He continues to prod me in the direction He needs me to go. Along the way, my faith has strengthened along with my love of God. Each day I awaken to new and meaningful blessings perceived by my trained senses.

For a time, it appeared as though my life would be complete. I had a stable job at Walmart. I had a steady companion to spend time with and share many laughs. I planned to spend the rest of my life with Angel. Additionally, I had the ambition to continue my efforts to pursue a legal career. I maintained faith, believing that God would direct me to my final destination. I seemed to have managed to overcome life's stresses and adversity. However, what was my perception did not exactly coincide with God's will. I continued to work third shift at Walmart. Without transportation I also walked about half a mile back and forth from my Connersville apartment to Walmart. These factors provided a barrier to my continued relationship with Angel.

The stability in my life continued through my birthday in 2016. On that date, Angel and I took a relaxing and exciting trip. Our first stop was the Walmart in Hamilton, Ohio. Selfishly, it was there where I purchased an item included in my new plan. I bought myself a new computer. This purchase was especially important for a few reasons. I would have easier access to study new legal developments. I had also been pondering writing books; one topic included the decline of morality in my lifetime. The computer would provide an easier way to achieve this objective. I would also have the ability to apply for other employment options when they became available. Finally, it would supply a much-needed source of entertainment and relaxation.

From Hamilton, we journeyed to two other places. The first was Jungle Jim's International Market in Fairfield, Ohio; Jungle Jim's is an enormous grocery store with the largest variety of items you could imagine. The second stop was a restaurant for a bite to eat. Although I felt I had selfish purposes in what we did that day, Angel had truly made that day memorable by sacrificing her time and vehicle for this trip. Unfortunately, this trip was the beginning of the end of my romance with Angel. I know this trip took a lot of energy from her. Although she went through chemotherapy treatments and finally her cancer was in remission, a lot of energy was required for moments like this. As a result, she began to tire of her relationship with me.

I began to realize my job and lack of a car were beginning to weigh heavily on Angel and our relationship. Working third shift is extremely difficult on relationships. I even told Angel that if anything were to tear apart our romance, it would be the hours I worked. Moreover, the moods I found myself in when we went out truly interfered with the enjoyment of those moments. Angel also spent a lot of time driving us to where we wanted to go. She was beginning to get frustrated and tired of this arrangement. I am sure she longed for someone to take the helm and drive her out on a date. While I assured her that my own car and a different job were in our future, that sentiment did little to allay her stresses. Surprisingly, these stresses reached a climax on Thanksgiving Day 2016. Angel and I were sitting in the car, talking. It was then that she indicated she desired to break up with me. She wanted to remain friends; however, she mentioned the drain my life was having on hers. In the recesses of my mind, I felt she was right. We needed to part and go our separate ways.

While that news was difficult, I knew God would see me through and continue guiding me along His chosen path. I continued working for Walmart. I walked to and from work. No longer with a companion, I spent time on my new computer reading about law and watching movies. Although Angel was no longer in my daily life, we cared about each other and maintained good thoughts and memories.

I have learned that while I may be complacent with my life at times, God will act in subtle yet bold ways to compel the action He desires. From the end of 2016 to June of 2018, I continued working and walking back and forth to Walmart. My savings increased significantly. I did not have the expense of a car, nor did I have the day-to-day expenses maintaining a relationship incurred. Unfortunately, my career at Walmart would come to a sudden and abrupt end.

Early on a Saturday morning in June 2018, I was called into the manager's office at Walmart. I was informed by an assistant manager that my job position was eliminated. I was given two options: either accept a new position with a 4:00 a.m. to 1:00 p.m. shift or leave. The management did not provide any significant details of what was happening or how the new process would work. Faced with this ultimatum, I provided a two-week notice and left the company that had offered me such stability through the years.

Like many times in the past, new anxiety appeared, resulting from the stress of how I would sustain myself financially. Yet I knew God would provide the blessings for me to survive. He had brought me out of dark circumstances throughout my past. My confidence in my faith meant there was no fear, for God would rescue me this time as well.

It almost brings me to tears when I relate the many times God has stood next to me. What may have been a discouraging defeat, He has snatched a victory from evil's lurking jaws. There can always be positives gleaning from adversity. There continues to be a divine reason God wants me to go down this path.

After I left Walmart, I needed to maintain my finances to keep a roof over my head and food in my stomach. For a brief period, I tried insurance sales. I received my Indiana life and health insurance license in July 2018. However, because these positions were commissioned-based, I did not have the time nor the finances to invest in training to achieve an income. It was clear I needed an income immediately.

During my transition away from Walmart to a possible insurance career, I immediately perceived the necessity of obtaining a reliable car. I had $7,500 saved at that time. With such significant savings, I knew I would be able to locate and purchase a decent vehicle. God then placed this opportunity right in front of my eyes. I had heard of a reliable used car dealership in Richmond, Indiana. They offered needed financing and a generous selection of quality vehicles. My only question was how I would be able to get to this dealership. A former Walmart associate and friend would provide the ride: Destiny. Destiny transported me to this location: JD Byrider. JD Byrider offered me a deal I could not refuse for a 2011 Chevrolet HHR. As I had a substantial amount for a down payment ($2,500), my obligation per week was much lower than I imagined. Once again, I was able to create a blossoming flower from a meager seed through work and frugality. More importantly, I did not realize the major significance this purchase would have for my future. God would open a door that would have serious ramifications for me to this day.

After leaving Wal-Mart, I drafted a résumé and began submitting applications for employment. I had never guessed the type of employment I would eventually obtain.

Modern technology is such a vital and wonderful thing. In my attempts to find employment, I saw ads for drivers for new tech businesses like Uber and Lyft. Realizing my need for an immediate income, I applied to be considered for a driving opportunity. With a good reliable vehicle along with a clean driving record and no license restrictions, both Uber and Lyft approved my application. I began driving for Uber and Lyft in August 2018 in the Indianapolis vicinity. It was as enjoyable and enlightening an experience as I could ever imagine. I have always enjoyed traveling. Moreover, I enjoyed meeting and talking to the individual riders. The opportunity was as rewarding as any opportunity I have had in my life, including practicing law. This experience led to future employment and a job and wage I never guessed I would obtain. Despite a brief absence from driving from September 2018 to January 2019 when I was employed at the New Castle Correctional Facility in the kitchen, I returned to driving in January 2019. However, with a fear of vehicle maintenance issues, I also applied for other stable full-time opportunities. I needed to guarantee myself a set income while monitoring the wear and tear on my vehicle.

My prayer for a suitable position was answered shortly thereafter in February 2019. SugarCreek is a meat packaging plant located in Cambridge City. They called me in for an interview. While they would temporarily utilize me in production, the opportunity would develop for me to become a van driver for this company. I openly accepted this opportunity and challenge. The wage was more than I would have ever imagined (eighteen dollars per hour). While my hours would fluctuate, I could expect twenty-four to twenty-nine hours weekly. With this opportunity, God truly put a monumental blessing in my life.

I started driving in May 2019. I drive a twelve-person employee shuttle van back and forth to Connersville and Indianapolis. I continue to be employed and drive for SugarCreek at the current time. While I continue to be approved to drive for Uber and Lyft, I have not driven for those companies for months now. God has blessed me in a way I had never expected.

For me, God exists and is real. He is there from your finest hours to your gloomy moments. He will be there to deliver you from your darkest hours. My testimony adheres to that belief. From early in my life, I thought I would eventually become an attorney and practice law. However, God took me down His path, which was developing my faith and unrelenting love for Him. While I do not practice currently, God provides for my financial and emotional security. Most importantly, my love for Him grows with each passing moment. I may never practice law again. If that is the case, my life has been a learning experience where I realize the awesome power of faith. God's true love has found me and will exist in my mind and heart forever.

CHAPTER 14

LIVING GOD'S MISSION: WHERE GOD CAN TAKE YOU

This photo of the author, Frank D. Tigue, was taken
by his computer camera circa June 2018.

I have lived an exceptional life. I was blessed in my youth to be raised by a faithful and hardworking father and a loving mother. I have a brother with whom I played and spent time with. I had a large family that was a healthy diversion. Most importantly, my entire family had much love to give. Along with my family, I had friends and teachers who taught me about life and how to live. This connection enabled me to excel in my studies and graduate not just high school but also college and law school too. My ambition to succeed was fueled by these interactions.

My faith in God was never lost along the way. Gradually, I began to realize some force more powerful than me was at work in my life. Simple events such as when the little girl asked me for my autograph compelled the thought that I was being watched and taken care of. Although unpleasant, my mishap with the little dog in Hot Springs taught me that God can bless even in the worst of circumstances. With this faith and love of God, I arrived at the conclusion that God did not want me to practice law for an extended time. He was more concerned with my discovery of the true love that had eluded my grasp throughout my life. That void was vivid and enormous after the death of my parents. Through time God was pulling me closer to Him.

Through it all, my faith in God and his blessings dictated the course my life would take. Gradually, these blessings occurred in His time, not mine. For example, I never looked back and complained after I relocated to Arkansas or when I closed my law office. I also did not complain when I walked to and from Burger King or when I was employed at the Connersville Walmart. I understood that God's hand and my strengthening belief provided for my needs.

God started to answer my prayers more frequently after a visit from His littlest messenger. I relocated to a place I always call home. I visited John and Darrell on a few occasions. Most importantly, He provided me with a very enjoyable job where my financial worries significantly diminished. That position was possible after God's hand, with my job elimination, forced me to purchase a much-needed vehicle. With these instances, what was lost along the way was my prayer that God would send me my true love who was missing in my life. He answered this prayer in His way when the bond between

Him and me began to solidify like the hardest of rock. Personally, for a brief period, I believe He even answered my prayer for that true romantic love I had requested.

While my relationship with Angel was short, there was no other person in my life whom I had the quality of time like with Angel. Furthermore, we traveled and spent many moments laughing and enjoying each other's company. She had been such an exceptional, caring, and compassionate person. For that brief period, I believe I got as close to true love as I had ever experienced during my entire life.

I used the past tense above. Angel and I continued to maintain occasional contact after we split. Unfortunately, on Monday, June 3, 2019, I received a text from Angel's sister-in-law, Charity. This text sadly informed me that Angel was in the hospital. Her cancer had returned and was very aggressive. The prognosis was that she had only one to three days to live.

I had never seen death firsthand. However, Angel was my dear friend and I needed to be with her in this time of need. I drove to the hospital. For the longest time, I held her hand and talked to her. Gradually, her breathing slowed and, finally, it stopped altogether. In that instant, I was glad I spent that last breath with her. While I was saddened by this moment, I understood God had even greater plans for her. Angel had been instrumental in my move to Connersville, purchasing my computer, and indirectly contributing to me obtaining my vehicle.

In conclusion, I implore the reader to search in your heart. You must take the time to review your past and present. Whether you believe or not, I believe this review will provide indicators (perhaps very indistinct) that God's mighty hand is at work with you as it had been with me. Most likely, God is paving a path for you and your life.

Once you understand the forces at play, you will undoubtedly be able to discern the path God desires for you to travel. Rest assured, once you embark on this journey, your love for God will grow like mine. Furthermore, you will begin to understand the power faith has to bless you with what you need. As a result, your life will be altered and improved. Walking with God is like no greater love than you can find. The power of faith and the love of and for God will truly find you as it has me.

SUNRISE (VALENTINE'S DAY, 2016)
This breathtaking photo was actually taken by me on Valentine's Day, 2016. Angel and I were on our way into Walmart in Connersville, IN when we caught a glimpse of something surreal. The sun was rising, but it was unlike any sunrise we had ever seen. We were in awe and started taking pictures. I truly believe this was another sign by God that He wanted me to take heed and pay attention to my life. I believe this image was one of God's actual presence.

CHAPTER 15

GOD'S GRACE CONTINUES

God's strength in your life only becomes more prevalent when you totally give your trust to Him. God will continue to guide you down the paths you will never think are possible. While not every event will be positive and favorable, God's grace will provide the energy, comfort, and strength to persevere even in the worst of times. Subtle occurrences will provide clues on the direction God wants to take you. For me, my driving position with SugarCreek provided a lot of comfort and financial security.

However, for some time I began to realize God had desired me to be a voice for Him. With the circular route my life had taken along with the ultimate discovery of the true love I had for Him, I had to convey that message to those receptive and willing to listen. Hence, I decided to memorialize my story in an autobiographical account of my life.

I was hired at SugarCreek on February 20, 2019. I began working part-time as a production associate; however, I received the offer to drive the company van in May. I transport employees back and forth from Connersville and Indianapolis. While this experience has been very rewarding, specific events occurred that left me little doubt concerning God's attention in my life. Before I first started driving the van, I was concerned my part-time hours might not be able to meet my financial obligations. Therefore, I made one trip a week to

Indianapolis to drive for Uber and Lyft. The income earned during that brief period was incredible. I made almost as much driving for a twelve- to sixteen-hour work stint as I made part-time at SugarCreek in a week. Unfortunately, my Uber/Lyft driving experience came to an abrupt halt in May 2019. I decided to drive Saturday evening to Sunday evening on Memorial Day weekend. Since the Indianapolis 500 was being held on Sunday, there was a terrific opportunity to earn money during that time. I now understand why it was referred to as the greatest spectacle in racing with the volume of fans in attendance.

I was very satisfied with my earnings that weekend. Likewise, I thoroughly enjoyed the people I assisted and the places I went to. However, I was headed toward my final destination that Sunday night to pick up my last rider. It was then that the unexpected happened. As I was driving and preparing to make a right turn, a vehicle pulled out and hit my car on the rear passenger door. I believe the driver was anticipating that I was preparing to turn into the convenience store she was exiting. While no one was hurt, it caused serious damage to my vehicle. I cannot begin to convey how low my heart dropped at this occurrence. This one accident created anxiety concerning my feeling as to the path God wanted me to go. I had never been involved in an accident of any kind prior to this one. The police were called; however, they never responded or took any kind of police report. My thought was because of the Indianapolis 500 earlier in the day, the police were busy responding to the aftermath of that event. I was covered by insurance that Uber provided. I was utilizing the Uber application at that time. However, before insurance paid, I had to be responsible for a one-thousand-dollar deductible.

I was able to return to Connersville and initiate contact with this insurance company. My claims representative was very helpful in assisting me in resolving this claim. I managed to take the car to a body shop for repairs. Additionally, I paid the one-thousand-dollar deductible with Uber's insurance company taking care of the rest. Hence, the repairs were timely made. However, that did not completely settle this accident.

I was hopeful that upon return of this deductible, I would utilize the proceeds to begin publication of a book. I started writing this book in May 2019 with its completion on September 3, 2019. I completed the rough manuscript on the anniversary of the same day I tripped over God's littlest messenger. While I never undertook an endeavor like publishing a book before, I realized its importance since God was orchestrating the direction of my life story.

Time passed, and I did not hear from the claims representative. Eventually, this representative called me and informed me that the other party was contesting the fault determination of the accident. Since I was constantly replaying that accident in my mind, I felt I followed all traffic laws. There was no way I could be determined to be at fault.

An arbitration hearing was scheduled for early January 2020. My heart sank. I was also thinking of the words my father used to say, "Hope for the best, but expect the worst." I was getting mentally prepared for the worst. I might not receive the return of this amount. I began to ask, "How can I financially afford publication of this book without this amount?"

In the fall of 2019, another barrier arose with my Chevrolet HHR. One day, as I was driving to work, the check engine indicator lit up on my dashboard. Initially, I was concerned. However, my concern got more intense when I noticed a different sound to my car's engine. This may be hard for the reader to understand. A car owner has an ear for when things are not quite right with his vehicle. I was able to take my car to JD Byrider's service department. Bob, the service manager, was able to discern the problem. I was sitting in a small waiting area when he came in and sat down. He showed me a part he had taken off the vehicle. I was not prepared for what he was going to tell me. He had some very devastating news. He told me my car needed another engine. As the timing mechanism was deteriorating, it was just a matter of time before the engine quit completely. My first thought was how I would pay for this repair. Soon thereafter, my heart sank as I no longer knew how I would pay for the publication of the book I so wanted completed.

Now my problems had grown astronomically again. I had to fix my car to get back and forth to work. Moreover, I wanted the return of my deductible to help offset the cost of any engine work. I really began to pray God would see me through this adversity.

God wants you to understand his grace and benevolence. He has a mighty hand that with one sweeping blow can change the complexion of any apparent misfortune. My consistent faith and prayers produced incredible and favorable results. Because of this, I will never waiver as to the power God has in my life, as long as I never turn away from my faith and love of Him.

Initially, I thought the car warranty contract through Car Shield I had purchased in April 2019 would help resolve the engine problem. However, that contract did not assist me the way I thought. I only had one recourse to assist in getting another engine: requesting a loan from my bank. I had genuine apprehension since my credit rating was destroyed after my second marriage to Jacqueline.

It is incredible how victory sometimes can be snatched out of the jaws of defeat. My visit to the bank for a loan did just that. When requesting the loan, I initially wanted to try to get my car paid off, and then I would repay the bank. However, I was informed that the value of my vehicle did not qualify me for that loan. Even so, there was also the possibility of a personal loan. After looking at my credit rating, I was informed that I would qualify for a $2,500 loan. (Incidentally, Bob told me the other engine would cost around $2,400.) The significant down payment to purchase my car and the steady, affordable biweekly payments I had been making helped produce an acceptable rating. I was ecstatic when I was told I would qualify for this loan.

God's continued grace had blessed me with a positive answer to the problem with my car engine. Additionally, Bob had overestimated the cost for the other engine. That amount was actually approximately

$1,600. My situation improved astronomically with my continued faith and prayers.

The last significant problem concerned whether I would receive the deductible from the Memorial Day auto accident. I kept praying God would provide a positive answer concerning the arbitration hearing. I also prayed that even if I did not receive a favorable outcome, that God would provide the comfort for me to accept the result that was forthcoming. I had a lot of anxiety concerning the outcome of the fault arbitration matter. It was late January, and I had not heard anything from my claims representative. However, I wanted the situation to play its way out. God would see that I would be contacted, regardless of the outcome.

God answered my prayers. It was about the last week in January when I received a call from my claims representative. She informed me she had just received the report from the arbitrator. The news was favorable. I would be receiving the amount of my deductible, directly deposited within the next few days.

With these two significant problems (deductible and car repair) resolved, I now had the resources to seriously pursue the publication of my book. My financial situation improved further with the direct deposit of a federal and state tax refund. It was just a matter of time before I would find a suitable publisher to make my dream of a book a reality.

While I am now on the verge of having my manuscript in print, I continue to have the desire to practice law. I have not lost sight of that possibility through the years. However, God has something more important that He wants me to pursue. When God sends a message (either clearly or implicitly), the recipient needs to pursue whatever God requires.

Once this autobiographical account of my life is published, maybe it is in God's plan for me to practice law again. I plan to follow whatever His intent is for me and my life. I have gotten to where I am by paying attention to the signals God gives me. I remain steadfast, loyal, and prayerful every day. God's grace will continue to impact me for the rest of my life.

To the readers of this account, God sincerely loves you. He will take you to extraordinary places. All you need to do is believe and understand He loves you and is willing to provide for your needs. Yet be patient because He hears and will answer prayers in His time and according to your needs. If you love Him back, God's grace can do extraordinary things in your life as He did mine.

CHAPTER 16

SOCIETY'S PATH: EVERYONE CAN FIND COMFORT THROUGH FAITH

With my life, God prepared me for the journey that my heart would take. This journey was personal for me. While He allowed me to practice law, He wanted me to understand and attach a greater significance to my life. He wanted me to find the true love existing between Him and me.

Ultimately, God wanted me to convey this feeling through the publication of a book chronicling my life's journey. Additionally, He wanted me to have readers individually assess their lives and the impact God had with them. He wanted me to make clear God loves everyone and will provide blessings to those in need. All these believers would have to do is understand, pray, and ask.

There is, however, an even more pronounced purpose behind the publication of this book. It consists of a request that society as a whole must hear. Society at large is in the midst of a moral crisis. Society needs to consider this writing and pursue the right path to align itself with God. It is not enough for people to attend church. These individuals need to actually attempt to live a righteous life.

They need to recognize their iniquities. It seems that people have lost their way through the years.

This sentiment was clearly evident with recent current events. In December 2019, a virus appeared in China. This virus (the coronavirus) had qualities that were never seen before. There was no known cure or vaccine for this newly existent disease. The lack of urgency and preparedness led to the eventual spread of this virus. The result was the imminent existence of a worldwide pandemic.

My life again experienced an upheaval on March 20, 2020. I had been continually driving the van for SugarCreek since May 2019. On March 20, I was informed that the van service would be discontinued at the plant. The main rationale was to help contain the spread of the virus. Like many adverse moments in my life, I began to have anxiety as to what direction my life would be going.

As of the time of this writing, this virus and pandemic has had deadly consequences. In the United States alone, more than fourteen thousand people have died from the illness caused by the virus. Furthermore, more than two hundred people have died in Indiana alone. At the time of this writing, these numbers have not reached their apex yet.

The true love of God, my faith, and my consistent prayers provided the answers and comfort I needed. I began to steadily pray that God would provide the blessings I need to survive this unprecedented crisis. My first concern was maintaining my economic viability. I needed to make sure I had a place to live and food to consume. Also, there was renewed sense of urgency concerning the need to publish my writing.

The mere fact of the creation of the virus provides the argument for the existence of God. This virus is so small that it cannot be seen with the naked eye. However, symptoms occurring leave no doubt that something vicious exists and is having a detrimental effect on our society. Just like the wind blowing through anyone's hair, people cannot see it. However, it is obvious that something is there. The existence of God operates on this principle. Every significant or extraordinary event cannot be explained away with scientific facts. Furthermore, life's events cannot be explained as simply coincidences. Like the wind and the virus, God exists, and is real, merely with how life happens for everyone. Hence, the presence of this virus in my lifetime is another serious aspect of my life compelling me to show people the extent of the need for faith on an even larger scale: for society and its welfare.

When I was informed the van would no longer be running, I received a blessing when I was also told that I would still be provided with some work at the plant. While the work hours would be significantly reduced, I would not be laid off at that time. Many areas in the country had stay at home orders, so of necessity, nonessential businesses would be temporarily closed. I needed to make sure that I had sufficient funds to meet my necessary obligations. Moreover, I wanted to make sure that publication of my manuscript would eventually occur.

God will always provide the answers to necessary questions when one needs them. While my work hours suffered, I also had the option of applying for unemployment insurance, should that assistance be needed. While I continued to have a lot of pride, I realized this help was warranted, especially during a moment of crisis our country was facing. Congress also passed an enormous stimulus package with increased unemployment benefits in an effort to avert a serious economic crisis during this pandemic. Another stimulus package would also include one-time payments to individual taxpayers. These facts provided significant comfort for me.

During the discontinuation of the van service, I have a very significant work responsibility. I have been entrusted with the responsibility to monitor individual worker and contractor temperatures upon arrival into the plant. While I only work approximately twenty-two to twenty-seven hours per week, I understand the significance of this responsibility. Nothing is more important than containing the spread of this new virus. A fever of over one hundred degrees is one of the first symptoms occurring in those having the infection.

With my faith and love of God, I realize that God will ultimately take care of me. My concern now is society as a whole. Violence in our country is commonplace. Anger, hatred, and bitterness have slowly permeated our country. Lies and possible corruption have also made an emergence in our lives. To love God and for Him to love us, our society needs to acknowledge these characteristics.

Biblical prophecy is clear that eventually the world is headed to an apocalyptic time. I believe, however, that with my love of God and God's love for me, we who believe can help avert immediate catastrophe. With this pandemic, I believe the answer is clear and simple. All society has to do is listen and act.

Society holds the answers to overcoming the virus crisis. Our country has moved away from God and faith. We have become a country of apathy, ignorance, selfishness, greed, and complacency. Our motivations have moved away from faith to a materialism that has never existed before. This materialism stands in conflict to God's love and the lives He desires for us. Upon request, God will provide society what it needs, not necessarily what it wants.

Society needs to restore its spiritual base. Society needs to restore its faith in God. This base is what allowed our country to maintain its strength since its founding. People need to come together to a common ground to reach compromises to significant problems. Advances in our lives have occurred because people cared enough to work together for the common good. We need to communicate as well as try to return to those days.

This book shows what power God has in my life when I firmly trust my heart and soul to Him. If society starts to feel this love, think how better all of our lives would be. God loves us, and He can do great things if we just believe. As a society, is it not worth the effort to have this faith and see what great things can happen?